BEING THE BEST YOU CAN BE IN MLM

"The energy and enthusiasm of John's in-person seminars and workshops leap out at you from the pages of this book. This is a 'must read' for the serious Network Marketing distributor."

Peter Kenyon and Malcolm J. Nicholl
Co-founders
Uni-Vite International

"John's professional and ethical teachings makes one proud to be in the MLM/Network Marketing industry. Anyone can follow these proven and practical principles. Everyone that does will become the best they can be... inspiring and powerful!"

Doris Wood
President
MLMIA (Multi-level Marketing International Association) and Executive Consultant for TWIG

"Once you read *Being The Best You Can Be In MLM*, you can't help but feel good about yourself, your business, and how to make it all work for you. Being a sponsor and advocate of John's seminars and workshops for years... this book is an affordable hands-on reference that everyone should own."

Sharon and John Farnsworth
Executive Directors (Top 5)
Sunrider International

"John Kalench's incisive book provided me with tremendous insight into our dynamic industry. It's written in a lively style full of useful recommendations and is worthwhile reading by anyone involved in Network Marketing. I applaud his work!"

J.F. Robert Bolduc
Co-Founder/Co-Chairman
Matol Botanical International
Chairman, MLMIA
(Multi-level Marketing International Association)

"You'll want to refer to *Being The Best You Can Be In MLM* time and time again. It's fun, easy reading with great stories and countless lessons to be learned."

Tom "Big Al" Schreiter
Author
The Big Al Series

"John's book captures the very *heart* of Network Marketing. No other book that I know of so completely and enjoyably lays out the path to success in our business. Light Force is proud to add a copy of *Being The Best You Can Be In MLM* in every one of our New Distributor Kits. Thank you, John, for this wonderful contribution to our dynamic industry!"

Pope McElvy
Vice-President
The Light Force Company

First Edition / September 1990

Fifth Printing / October 1991

Text and cover design by Jim Schmal

BEING THE BEST YOU CAN BE IN MLM

How To Train
Your Way
To The Top In
Multi-Level/Network Marketing–
America's Fastest-Growing Industry

BY JOHN KALENCH

Acknowledgements

Thanks a million to Carolyn, Jeff, Betty, Bob, Katherine, Carol, Jim, and especially John (JMF). Special friends that have made a special difference in this book—and even more importantly, in my life!

And a special, heart-felt thanks to my main-man, my best man, Tom. From the very beginning, through thick and thin, you've been by my side. I can't begin to tell you how much your loyalty, faith, trust and service has meant to me. Please know that I appreciate and love you for all you've done—and all you are!

To my beautiful wife Yvonne—thanks for choosing me. This book is dedicated to you, sweetie!

Contents

Foreword

Being The Best You Can Be in MLM... is that what you really want?

Please, think about this for a moment. Do you really want to be *the best* you can possibly be?

If your heart-felt and well-thought-out answer is, "Yes!"—then I can unconditionally guarantee you that John Kalench's book will help you do that.

Being The Best You Can Be in MLM is about you and your future in the most extraordinary and exciting business in the world.

You'll begin by taking a look at the *why* of your business. John will guide you through a process where you will uncover your life's purpose, and establish a set of powerful, compelling goals in pursuit of that purpose. You'll then learn how to use the *four forms of fuel* to charge your purpose and goals with potent, creative energy.

Then, prepare yourself for an artfully crafted journey of self-discovery. You'll learn proven, practical "things to do" that will empower you to build and live a personal and professional life that outshines your most cherished desires and aspirations. This book is filled with promises and possibilities—for you!

The possibility of accomplishing all your life goals. . . of experiencing a richly rewarding, creative and fulfilling career... of developing your highest human potential... of generating the real and tangible experience of financial freedom... and of contributing to other people in a unique and special way.

As for the promises...? That's the best part. *Being The Best* actually shows you *how* to achieve all of this!

John takes you step-by-step through *every* aspect of creating *and keeping* a successful MLM/Network Marketing business of your own. You'll discover prospecting tips and telephone skills that you can immediately put into action! You'll learn how to make dynamite presentations and hold "opportunity showcases" that are professional and generate results. You'll also find ways to skillfully "answer" objections and how to use a proven follow-up system that will provide a strong customer base and a steady flow of new people into your business. Whether it's in-home meetings, new distributor training, or duplicating your efforts effortlessly—you'll find it all here!

John Kalench speaks with the understanding voice of a decade of experience. He's been where you are, and he knows what works and what doesn't. On the "street-smart" side, John knows his stuff inside-out. He's built a successful million-dollar MLM distributorship, created and directed his own Network Marketing corporation, and through his company, Millionaires In Motion (MIM), has trained more than 5,000 men and women to become successful Network Marketers. In support of their work, MIM received the "Presidents Award for Training Excellence" from the Multi-Level Marketing International Association, (MLMIA), for two consecutive years. Yes, John *is* a master trainer of business building skills.

John has taken all the mystery out of this enigmatic and complex business of ours. Many times throughout your reading, you'll put the book down and exclaim to yourself, "Wow!—that's great!"...or..."So that's how you do that!" I have read almost every book written about this business. Some were better than others, but none is as caring and complete as this one.

It's comprehensive, compassionate, powerful, practical, and filled with dozens of "Ah Ha" revelations you'll want to apply to your business immediately. The style is personal, enjoyable and fun to read. It's like having John as a close friend, sitting in your living room, sharing his knowledge and experience so that you may learn.

I have been praying for the definitive book on Network Marketing for years...and I love John Kalench for writing it. I think so much of *Being The Best You Can Be in MLM* that I'm giving a copy of it—*free*—to every subscriber of our newsletter! It is a *must* for everyone who is serious about succeeding in this business.

The best way to use it is to read it yourself many times, and to get a copy into the hands of every new distributor in your Network before the ink dries on their distributor application. If you do that, I guarantee your MLM success.

John Fogg
Editor
MLM Success™

How To Use This Book

This book is different from others you may have read, and you may want to approach it differently.

I have some suggestions on how to use this book I'd like you to consider.

First, don't be intimidated by the sheer quantity of information it contains. It represents over a decade of teaching and training experience with thousands of people.

I don't expect you to sit down and read it from cover to cover all in one shot. There may be some of you who will. Most of you won't—and that's okay. Sir Francis Bacon said, "Some books are to be tasted, others to be swallowed, and some few to be chewed and digested."

This book is the kind to be "chewed and digested." It's the same difference between giving you a fish and feeding you for a day, or teaching you how to fish so you can feed yourself for a lifetime. Fishing takes time to learn and master. And what I'm up to here is having you become a master fisherman or fisherwoman. So take your time.

Second, this is a "user friendly" book. I don't consider myself a writer. I prefer to talk. So this is a talking book. Look at it as a conversation between you and me. That's what I mean it to be.

Third, this book is what they call "pro-active." That means a *How To* book. The principles I teach you here are all time-tested and people-proven—so don't think of yourself as a guinea pig.

Read "Your Introduction" and Chapters One and Two first. Do them in one shot, if you can make the time. Do all the exercises—force yourself if you have to. This will put you in touch with the all-important *why* of your doing this business. The *why* is a must and there's no way of getting around it when you're serious about *Being The Best You Can Be In MLM!*

Then, take the remaining chapters one at a time. Read them, learn what to do in the various aspects of your MLM/Network Marketing business and put the principles and techniques into practice yourself. By the way, for the reasons of both simplicity and consistency, from this point on I'll refer to the Multi-level Marketing (MLM) or the MLM/Network Marketing industry as only Network Marketing. They are one and the same and a matter of personal choice. So we'll use what is considered the more progessive term—Network Marketing.

No matter what you discover in each chapter, I know you'll encounter two, three, or more, wonderful "Ah Ha's." These are the great ideas that get equally great results. Use them and see what happens for yourself. And as you experience them working for you, share them with the other men and women in your network.

You don't have to wait until the whole system comes together in the New Distributor Training (Chapter Ten) before you begin to teach the various parts to others. That's the point of the entire book.

"We teach best that which we need most to learn."

Fourth, do you know the story of the young man on a New York street corner who asked a famous violinist for directions on how to get to Carnegie Hall? The great man's answer was, "Practice, practice, practice!"

Same here. This book is a treasure chest of good ideas—that's what it's *meant to be*. It comes to life only when you use it.

Knowledge isn't power until it's combined with action. It's kind of like the story of the old sailor who was asked... "If a man fell off this pier into the water, would he drown?" And the old sailor replied... "Falling into the water doesn't drown the man—staying there does."

So, read this book and immediately take what you've learned and act! I know the principles work—I've helped thousands of people use them successfully for years— but you don't know that yet. And the only way you'll know it is to try them out for yourself. Then, as the saying goes, "If it works—keep doing it."

I have another suggestion: once you've completed reading this book—read it again. And then read it one more time. The third time is the charm. If you read this book twenty times, I promise you'll still learn something new.

And finally, "work smart" by putting this book to work for you in your business!

Each time you sponsor a new distributor, have them read "Your Introduction" and Chapters One and Two before they go through your New Distributor Training Program. When they understand *why* they want to do this business, teaching them the *how to's* will be simple. This proven method will get them, and your relationship, off to a fast, rock-solid start.

Then, as they continue with each chapter and begin practicing the principles themselves, you'll find you've started a powerful system of duplication that can't be beaten.

It's the key to achieving financial freedom in the surest, fastest way possible. And that's what *Being The Best You Can Be In MLM* is all about!

Have a great time!

Your Introduction: Understanding Network Marketing– You've Got To Love It!

How would you like to open up vast new horizons of unlimited possibilities for your life? You would? Great! Well, here's how: Fall in love with Network Marketing. I'm not talking about loving it for the money, and I don't mean thinking it's "a pretty neat idea," either. I'm talking about really being in love. When you love this business as much as you do your product and company, your success is inevitable! Just what is there to love? That's what this Introduction is all about.

I t was more than ten years ago that I was introduced to this industry for the very first time.

I was invited to the home of a friend to what I now know was an "opportunity meeting." I sat there and listened to a man talk about a company and a product, and then he went into explaining an opportunity which way back then they only called Multi-level Marketing (MLM).

He drew a bunch of circles on the board. That was the first time I had ever seen those circles. You know the ones: this circle is you, and these five circles are the people you personally sponsor... and these 25 circles represent... and so on "down-the-line."

Well, I was literally *blown away!*

All the way home, I just couldn't get those circles out of my mind. I was so excited I thought I was going to explode. I'd never been so enthusiastic about anything before *in my entire life!*

WHAT'S IT ALL ABOUT?

It wasn't the company that excited me. It wasn't the products that turned me on, either. And it wasn't the possibility of, "After all these years in a dead end job, here, *at last*, was a chance for me to be successful." I was already a success—in fact, my medical business was growing bigger and more successful every year.

That wasn't it. It was this: For the first time in my life I'd been shown a business system that made complete and total sense to me.

Here was a way to achieve everything I ever wanted in life—*by helping others!* Here was a way that my success in life could be directly proportionate to the level *of service and support I provided for other people.* Incredible!

I lay there in bed that night looking up at the ceiling, and the whole thing turned into this huge window of possibilities. All night long, I thought about how this extraordinary new system of *truly* free enterprise and opportunity would allow me to become the very best person I could possibly be... and make the biggest and most positive difference with other people I could ever want to make in my life.

I knew, laying there in bed wide-eyed and electrified, that this was what I would do for the rest of my life.

A LIFETIME GOAL

I knew it was important for me to establish a goal—a lifetime goal—that would help me focus my energy and optimize this whole new adventure. I thought and thought all night long. By the time the sun came up—I had it.

My lifetime goal is: *Before I die, I want to have one million friends.*

Every single day since that long and wonderful night over ten years ago, that's what I have strived for. I know beyond a shadow of a doubt, as I focus on that goal, that every other thing in my entire life takes care of itself *perfectly.*

I have no concerns at all about money. As long as I've been focused on having one million friends, money has taken care of itself. Are you familiar with the book

entitled, *Do What You Love And the Money Will Follow?*
Well, I do what I love and, yes, the money *does* follow!

I'm rarely concerned about decisions, either—what to
do in this situation or that one. My life's choices are
automatic. If they serve my goal of having one million
friends—I do it! If not—I don't. It's fantastic!

The reason I was enabled (and truly empowered) to
establish such a goal was that for the first time in my life,
I had found a system that actually made that gigantic goal
real and tangible for me. Please understand what I'm
saying here. Before I knew Network Marketing existed,
the goal that so powerfully and *effortlessly* drives my life
today was absolutely unthinkable... even unimaginable.

Network Marketing is what made it possible!

WHAT IS NETWORK MARKETING REALLY OFFERING YOU?

My point in sharing this with you is not to encourage you
to have a goal of one million friends—although if you
want to do that, that would be super.

My point is that Network Marketing is such a unique
and extraordinary system that I firmly believe it will open
up for you—as it did for me and has for thousands of
others just like us—a vast new horizon of possibilities for
your life. Once you begin to grasp the unlimited potential
of Network Marketing, you'll begin to reveal your deepest
desires and aspirations. Those desires and aspirations
that you simply hadn't allowed yourself to ever consider.

Why? Because Network Marketing actually makes
the impossible possible.

How?

Network Marketing drives people toward their destinies. It naturally accelerates your learning curve. It enables you to grow as a person faster and farther. It enables you to accomplish more and to contribute more to yourself and your world. Network Marketing is a system that provides you the opportunity to leverage your unique, God-given creative abilities to have a dramatic, beneficial impact on the lives of hundreds, thousands, or even *millions* of other people! And it does this by virtue of its own inherent, powerful and inspired natural design.

Let me explain what I mean.

THE TRUTH ABOUT NETWORK MARKETING

No other support system of which I am aware—in business, sports, relationships, etc.—so completely honors the freedom and responsibility of the individual.

From your very first day in Network Marketing you are free!

You choose with whom you want to work—with which company, what products or services you represent, and how you will work with them. *You choose* when you work: the days, the hours. *You choose* where you work: from your home, an office, or while traveling. *You choose* your style of working: person-to-person, through the mail, over the phone, in small groups or with huge gatherings of people. Every single aspect of your business is up to you. *It's your choice because it's your business.*

Your Network Marketing business is unhampered by the vast majority of common functional and financial business concerns. The company you work with as an independent contractor handles them for you. Capitalization, administration, accounting, data processing, product development, purchasing, all aspects of production, packaging, marketing including the design and implementation of the compensation plan and the production of sales support materials, warehousing, shipping... all this and more is the company's job—*not yours!*

So what is your job? Great question!

Your job is to do the following three things:

1. USE THE PRODUCTS AND LOVE THEM

There's no short-cut—and it's a good thing, too! Network Marketing offers some of the most extraordinary products and services in the world. This business is filled with one-of-a-kind, state-of-the-art, fantastic products that get the most amazing results for the people who use them.

Products that help people lose weight and keep it off—people who've rarely been able to diet successfully before. Nutritional and health products that help the human body relieve symptoms of disease and discomfort, while providing the kind of increased energy and mental clarity that actually changes people's lives.

In Network Marketing you can find personal and household products that do the impossible. Cleaners, deodorizers, shampoos, soaps, toothpaste and more, that out-perform common supermarket and drug store items so remarkably, you have to use them yourself to actually believe what a superior value they are.

There are discount phone services that can save you a small fortune. Things you can bolt on or pour into your car that increase gas mileage and horsepower—and help the environment in the process!

Network Marketing has created the home water filtration business—a $1 billion industry that makes a living removing impurities from your water! There are Networking services and memberships that enable ordinary people to participate in investments, travel and many other benefits previously available only to the rich and famous.

There is no end to the list of remarkable products and services offered through Network Marketing. Our business has some of the highest quality, most amazing products and services the world has ever seen!

So Point #1 should be easy to do—love your product. Be your own best customer—and with that, you have a classic win-win situation!

2. SHARE AND RECOMMEND YOUR PRODUCT TO OTHERS

This is so simple. You do this all the time. We all do. We can't help it unless we choose to go through life as an "undercover agent!"

When we see a terrific movie or go to a great restaurant, we naturally tell people about it. How did you decide on the TV you own, the car you drive, the neighborhood where you live? You talked to other people—more than likely friends that shared their experience with you. They told you about their favorite brand of this or that. You took in these recommendations and then made decisions.

Professional marketers know they have to do three things to guarantee lasting success:

1) They have to get you to try their product. That's called "trial."

2) They have to get you to use their product or service again and again. When you do, they call you a "consumer franchise."

And the most important of all... the thing all marketers dream of accomplishing:

3) They need to have you like it so much, you recommend it to other people. It's called "consumer advocacy."

Network Marketing companies simply reward you directly for your consumer advocacy. They understand the value of your P.O.P. (Point of Purchase) recommendations to others. So, Network Marketing companies choose to compensate you, the individual marketer.

It's almost like being paid to be a friend. Friends share good news with each other. Discovering a fantastic product or service with wonderful benefits is something you share with your friends. In Network Marketing, you are paid for doing this. Think of it as "thank you" money. And the more friends you develop, the greater your potential, contribution and rewards.

3. SPONSOR OTHER PEOPLE TO JOIN YOU
When people see you having fun building your own business... that it's simple... that you're making money... that the people in your Network and company are

actively helping you... they'll think very seriously about joining you.

Network Marketing isn't about "twisting someone's arm" or "hard-selling" anyone to do anything. It's about offering it to people and letting them make a choice. This isn't the persuading or convincing business. It's the *sorting* business. You just keep offering until you find the right person at the right time. That's it.

You sponsor as many or as few people as you choose. When you do, you agree to be responsible for teaching them how to do what you do—and what you teach are these three steps.

1. Use the product and love it.
2. Share it with other people.
3. Sponsor others into the business.

IT'S ALL UP TO YOU

The standards of success for your business are your own. No one measures your performance but you. There is no supervisor or boss telling you what to do, how or when to do it.

Your ethics and attitudes also are all your own. The thoughts and feelings you have are directly expressed in the outcomes you produce. You are rewarded honestly and sometimes richly in direct proportion to your values and the efforts you put forth. There isn't anything or anyone in this industry to prevent you from "just gettin' by" or from "soaring like an eagle" to the very highest pinnacle of success. *It's all up to you.*

No one with more advanced education, inherited

wealth, a more supportive environment, with "born talent,"or with any other so-called social or economic advantage has a better chance than you do of succeeding in Network Marketing.

In this business, we are all born completely equal.

In this business, we all succeed based solely upon how we balance our freedoms with our responsibilities.

HOW YOU VIEW NETWORK MARKETING

One of the people I have the highest respect for in this business is K. Dean Black, Ph.D. In his exceptional pamphlet, "The MLM Simple Success Guide," he offers one of the most concise and clear explanations of what makes Network Marketing work. Here is part of Dr. Black's explanation:

> When people aren't succeeding, when they feel frustrated, angry or discouraged, it's often because they aren't seeing things as they really are. When they clear up their seeing, when they see the truth, they succeed, and they feel happy.
>
> Successful distributors see the truth about four things: (1)(Multi-level [Network] Marketing; (2) the company; (3) themselves; and (4) other people. Unsuccessful distributors often get blocked because they're not clear about one or more of these four things.
>
> **Seeing the Truth About Multi-level [Network] Marketing**
>
> Some people don't like Multi-level Marketing, but there's nothing wrong with the principle, just with the way some people work with it.
>
> Here, for example, are the facts about the multi-level principle:

Fact 1: Multi-level or pyramid structures are for distributing. Above a certain size any organization that distributes products or services ends up shaped like a pyramid, with multiple levels that get bigger as you go down. Delegation creates a multi-level pyramid. Our government is also a multi-level pyramid. So are our schools and churches. All successful businesses, because they distribute products and services, end up shaped like a multi-level pyramid.

Fact 2: In any multi-level structure, the power comes from the bottom. Our government distributes services down a pyramid, but we give it power from the bottom, with our votes. Marketing companies distribute products down a pyramid, but we give them power from the bottom, with our dollars. So pyramids set up a flow that runs two ways: first down, then up. Value flows down the pyramid; power in response flows up. If value stops flowing down, power (in the form of dollars or votes) stops flowing up, and the system collapses.

Fact 3: Multi-level structures work only when responsibilities are handled at the lowest possible level. This was our founding fathers' idea. They said, in essence, what people can do for themselves, they must do. What we can't do for ourselves gets passed to the next higher level. We can't put in our own streets and sewers, for example, so the city does it. What the city can't do, the state does, and so on.

Whenever upper levels start doing what lower levels could do for themselves, the system starts to get cumbersome, and everything slows down and eventually collapses.

Multi-level Marketing is nothing more than a business system that puts responsibility at the lowest possible level, on individual people, and that's why multi-level companies can grow so fast. But it also means that no multi-level company is stronger than the character of its distributors.

Multi-level companies fail when their leaders or distributors forget that power flows up a multi-level structure only when genuine value flows down. When people seek money, in other words, without first giving value. The worst cases are the chain letter type "illegal pyramids," where the only value given is the right to recruit others, which is no value at all. In other cases, people may try to create the illusion of value by offering products that are not, in fact, the main purpose of the business, and that are worth less than the money they're asking for. Such illusions eventually get found out and when they do, the dollars stop flowing up the system, and the company collapses.

Multi-level companies also fail, or at best, get bad reputations, when their distributors lack character. Sometimes distributors recruit with deception. Sometimes they complain and backbite. Sometimes downline groups fight. Sometimes people spread rumors. These and similar human weaknesses often show up more easily in multi-level companies than in regular companies because multi-level companies leave people so free.

Whatever the cause, multi-level companies fail, not because of the multi-level principle, but because people don't support the principle with honesty and excellence. So have faith in the multi-level principle and take care to be honest and accept only excellence.*

HAVING FAITH IN THE NETWORKING PRINCIPLE
Just what does that mean?

It means honoring the natural structure. Dr. Black gives two more examples I feel are important to share with you:

If you see your customers and downline as sources of money, you probably won't do very well. They'll pick up on your self-centered interest and move away from it. On the other hand, if you see them as opportunities to serve and support, they'll pick up that as well and move toward it.*

"Opportunities to serve and support." I can't begin to tell you how absolutely vital this point is. If you get nothing else from this entire book but this one point, you will have the key to success in Network Marketing.

And one more from Dr. Black:

We feel either abundance or scarcity in our mind, open ourselves or defend ourselves accordingly, and create in that fashion a life that exactly mimics what we feel. So see life's abundance, and see how to create it for other people, as well as for yourself.*

Again, *"to create it for other people."* This is it, my friends. This is what will make Network Marketing work for you!

NETWORK MARKETING IS LIKE LIFE ITSELF

The same "natural structure" that supports and drives Network Marketing is the very same natural structure that empowers, nourishes and supports you in your life. That's why this unique form of business enterprise is so very special. It works the same way you do—it's a pure and perfect mirror of life itself.

What happens to you when you behave in a selfish or self-centered way? How do you feel about yourself and others? How well does your life work?

What happens when you are compassionate and

---

* "The MLM Simple Success Guide" by K. Dean Black, Ph.D. (Brerie Enterprises, Springville, UT), p. 1-5.

appreciative of others? How do you feel then? How well does your life work then?

In Network Marketing—as in life—the "feedback" loop is direct and unobstructed. Your success or failure in Network Marketing is directly of your own making.

You've seen what happens to nations, organizations and individuals that are led by greed, dishonesty, irresponsibility, fear... You know what's in store for them. As Dr. Black points out, people—and life itself—move away from them. The same future awaits Network Marketers driven by those qualities.

On the other hand, people, life and success move *toward* nations, organizations and individuals that "serve and support" them. Network Marketing does, too.

UNDERSTANDING NETWORK MARKETING

The number one reason for people not succeeding in this business is because they just don't understand it. They don't grasp its basic principles nor practice the simple "how to's" that make those principles real through action.

The big challenge here is that when you don't understand Network Marketing—how it really works and what *really* drives it—it's almost impossible to be in love with it. I believe that in order to succeed in Network Marketing, as with any life endeavor, *You've Got To Love It!*

That night ten years ago when I was first introduced to Network Marketing, I didn't really understand it. My head was swimming with possibilities, the implications, what it all meant. I *knew* I was on to something extraordinary, but what—how? I desperately wanted to understand.

I lay there wide awake, the ceiling of my room a cinematic panorama of possibilities, meanings and images flashing in front of me all night long! When the sun came up I knew what this business was all about. I understood it—and I loved it. Over the years I have been involved in this business, my love has grown and intensified into a bonfire of passion.

WHAT WILL IT TAKE FOR YOU?

You've Got To Love It! This is one of the very few instances where there just isn't any other way.

How can you do that?

Two ways: one is to *fall in love*—like love at first sight. That's what I did. But I also did it the second way as well. I *learned to love* it.

Through this book, I may be able to help you and the other men and women networking with you to fall in love with Network Marketing. I'm really not sure about that though, because it's so much more up to you than it is up to me.

Even so, *I have absolute faith that I will be able to show you how to learn to love this business.* That's my job. What I love to do is teach men and women just like you to be successful in Network Marketing. I've taught thousands of them already, and I'm on my way to my goal of having one million friends.

ARE YOU READY TO BEGIN?

You are? Great! First, let me tell you what we'll be doing.

THE PURPOSE OF THIS BOOK

Have you ever heard it said that "The best way to master a subject is to teach it?" It is absolutely, 100 percent true! Which is one of the very important reasons this is not a "*self-help*" book per se. It's a Network Marketing training book for you to use for *teaching and training your people to be successful!*

I know from experience with teaching thousands of people to be Network Marketing Teachers and Trainers that this approach is the fastest, most empowering way for them to master this business and be tremendously successful!

Throughout the book you'll be learning many new and valuable tools, tips and techniques you can use immediately to increase your own performance and productivity. I know you'll rush right out and try the information on using the telephone, or change the delivery of your next presentation.

That's great, and it's certainly what I intended. But for you the real value of this book is when you discover its secret. When you get to the point where everything falls into place and you grasp for the first time the simple, fun, systematic, duplicatable and extraordinarily powerful training program I'm teaching you.

THE BOOK IS DIVIDED INTO TWO MAIN SECTIONS

Chapters One and Two are about *why* you're doing this business. When you understand *why*, you're 90 percent of the way to the mastery of Network Marketing. You'll quickly learn that discovering this *why* is important for you to do with your people as well. And I'll teach you how to do just that.

The next seven chapters take you step-by-step through the fundamental aspects of *how* to do this business successfully. I'll go from Prospecting all the way through to conducting big Opportunity Showcase meetings. And along the way you'll have hundreds of new ideas you can use immediately to increase your own success and that of your people.

Chapter Ten, "New Distributor Training," will bring it all together and Chapter Eleven will show you how to Duplicate yourself over and over to grow a large and successful Network Marketing Organization. One that can provide you with a lifetime income that goes beyond financial *security* to real and lasting financial *freedom*!

Fair enough?

NOW, LET'S BEGIN

Oh, one more thing.

How will I know when you've truly mastered these principles and become an excellent Network Marketing Teacher and Trainer?

It's simple really—*you will be better at it than I am.*

Does that shock you a little? Don't let it. That's my job, and it's what every teacher in the world who is true to himself or herself is really up to.

I know that when my students surpass me—I've done it right! That's my goal with this book. The way I see it, a goal is a promise I make to myself. And if there's one thing I'm a fanatic about, it's keeping my promises.

So let's go find a comfortable spot where we can talk this through. I have all the things we'll need, with the exception of a quiet place, a notepad and a pencil. I'm counting on you for those items! And I want you to know, I am really looking forward to working with you. So what do you say we get started?

Chapter One:
Your Goals and Purpose

When you enroll people in your business, you should first help them establish their goals and purpose. Until you know the personal goals and purpose of your people, you can't connect your business opportunity with what's truly important to them in their lives. Aligning one's personal and professional goals with the freedom and power inherent in Network Marketing is the first step for creating success in this business.

I f you approach books like I do, you probably skipped by "How To Use This Book," and "Your Introduction: Understanding Network Marketing"—so as to get to the heart. I can appreciate your enthusiasm for wanting to get started quickly. The information in those sections, however, is vital to the overall message of this book. So please, take the time to read them. If you've already done so, then let's get started.

As a Network Marketing Trainer, I'm obviously very keen on the *how to*. One of the biggest challenges in our business is that so few of us were ever taught how to do it. The fundamental task of a Network Marketing sponsor and trainer is just like that of a good parent. As the song says, "Teach your children well."

However, no matter how vital and important the *how to* is, *why* must always come first. It's been said that mastery of any subject is ten percent how to do it and 90 percent why. When the *why* is in place, the *how* to becomes automatic.

Here's why that's true.

BEYOND GOALS

There's been a tremendous amount written and spoken about goals. In my intensive interaction with thousands of people in workshops, seminars and consultations over many years, I've begun to question this whole business of goal setting and goal getting.

The primary misunderstanding I see people having with goals is that too often they become the end result in themselves. They're not! A goal is actually something very different than that. A difference vital for you as a Network Marketing teacher and trainer to understand.

GOALS ARE FORMS OF ACKNOWLEDGMENT

Most of the time we establish our goals based on desired tangible results, such as things that money can buy or enable us to do or to be. We work very diligently on accomplishing these goals.

I've discovered that most goals, when achieved, don't give us the real fulfillment and satisfaction that we initially desired or thought that goal would actually bring us. I believe this happens because so many of us look at goals as the answer in life.

I suggest we look at goals a little differently.

I'd like you to consider goals not as the end result, but rather as "the means."

Look at goals as forms of acknowledgment that we deserve in our journey to achieving some higher purpose. I'm not real big on "keeping score." That speaks of comparison and competition with others. In reality, the only real standards we should use to judge ourselves are those higher values within ourselves to which we aspire—*not* by comparing ourselves to what others want, or want us to do, or seem to have accomplished themselves.

In one sense, achieving a goal is a self acknowledgment that we're on the right path to becoming the person we've always wanted to be.

Some call it the path of mastery.

IT'S YOUR PURPOSE

Back when we were kids, most of us realized we had special talents, skills, and desires that were unique to us. We knew that we were here to make a difference in a way that only we could make. Can you remember that?

Take a moment right now. Think back to a time when, as a child, you recognized that you were special. Focus on your own true beliefs about yourself and the realization of how special you really were.

Close your eyes and do that now. Just take a couple of deep breaths, relax completely, and allow yourself to remember some of those moments as a child. Perhaps it was during a game you played, a fantasy character you wanted to be "when you grew up," or a time when you were day-dreaming. Get in touch with those past thoughts and feelings now.

Great. Now I want you to realize that it's not important whether you wanted to be a fireman, a cowgirl, a great diplomat, an actor or an actress. What matters is the essence or feeling you'd have if you were actually living that dream. Let's "up-date" your sense of purpose that you just got in touch with and bring it to the *now*—this moment in your life.

WHAT IF ?

Here's a great exercise I use all the time. You'll need your personal copy of this book or a note pad and a quiet place and time to do this.

Get yourself relaxed again so your mind can flow easily and answer these three questions. Don't judge any of what you write down. Just write, no matter what comes up. No conditions. No limitations. Let your thoughts flow out on the paper.

1. If I didn't have to work for a living—what would I love to do? (To clarify—this question is about "Doing what you love.")

_____

_____

_____

_____

_____

_____

2. If I were just given $1 million, tax-free, what would be the first thing that I'd do with it? (Now please, do not say "pay off my bills." Of course you'd do that. Forget about _survival_. We're talking BIG prosperity here. I want you to stretch yourself and think of what you'd _really_ love to do with the money)

_____

_____

_____

_____

_____

3. If I learned that I had six months to live—what would I do with the rest of my life? (These are six *healthy* months. No pain or debilitating disease. What would you do?)

_____

_____

_____

_____

_____

When you've had the fun of completing this exercise, find the personal and quiet time to read and review all your answers carefully—and do that as soon as you possibly can!

Some of what you've written may seem ridiculous or just too outrageous to be real. That's fine. Some of what you've written may literally bounce off the page at you. That's great. What I want this exercise to reveal for you is the *essence*. What's at the heart of those things you wrote down.

A great question to ask yourself about any of what you wrote is, "If I did that, or had that, what would it bring me?"

You may need to ask that question of yourself a number of times for each answer you wrote down. And each time you answer it, like removing the outer layers of a fine pearl, you'll be getting closer and closer to the essence of your answer.

You'll know you've gotten to the essence when you simply can't answer the question any other way. When that happens, don't question any further. Just accept that answer and try it on for size. Then—if it's comfortable—wear it.

DREAMS AND ASPIRATIONS

The essence of the dreams you had as a child and that you revealed in this exercise, is an indication of the lifestyle you want to live and the person you aspire to become. These are keys to your true purpose. Please be very clear about this—*we all have a purpose.*

WRITE IT DOWN NOW

Before I ask you to write down your purpose, I want you to understand why you should write it down.

You've heard it said, "You are what you eat." Well, I'm not sure about that, but I am sure about this! *"You are what you think you are."*

Our thoughts are very powerful. They shape what comes into being in our lives. One way to focus your thoughts is to write them down.

Writing is a powerful action. By writing things down you make a commitment. You commit what you've written to your subconscious mind. When your commitment is expressed positively, and in the present-tense, your subconscious accepts it as an accomplished fact. Your subconscious mind will then guide every aspect of your life "as if" that purpose were true. Isn't that awesome?

Before you begin, let me share my purpose with you.

For all those who desire education and support in their pursuit of personal excellence and achievement, I commit myself to serve you. I promise to use compassion, integrity and example as my instruments. I do this lovingly, so as to contribute and to be happy and to prosper. Everything I do, every opportunity I look at, every action I take in my life, must be in alignment with my purpose. I know that as I pursue this purpose passionately, I will grow, and as I grow—so will my purpose. I will never fulfill it totally. I'll always be in pursuit of it. As a result I will achieve, do and be more than I ever have before—both for myself and for others.

A life's purpose is unending. It's not something you accomplish, then quit and retire. In fact, a good test for the truth of your prospective purpose is that if you can see an end to it, it's not your real purpose.

So take whatever time you need—right now—and write out in one or two paragraphs what you believe to be your life's purpose. If your written purpose is longer than one page, you probably can be more specific.

Choose your words well. Define your purpose as clearly, accurately and lovingly as you can. Go ahead—do it now.

MY LIFE'S PURPOSE—DEFINED

_____

_____

_____

_____

_____

_____

_____

_____

_____

_____

_____

_____

_____

_____

_____

_____

So, what do you think? How do you feel?

Let me share with you how I felt when I had (finally!) written down my purpose:

I was on a plane with my associate, Tom, flying to Minneapolis to conduct a two-day workshop. I had my pad of paper out and was working on my purpose. This was something I had intended to do for a long time. With Tom asleep in the seat next to me, it was the perfect time to get it done.

I wrote and wrote, trying to refine it, choosing my words with care. I was really working at it. It took me an hour and a half to write that one simple paragraph.

When I finally finished, I was exhilarated! I felt like I was going to explode. I jumped out of my seat. I couldn't contain myself. I certainly couldn't sit down! I was pacing the aisle back and forth with this huge grin plastered on my face. I wanted to rush up to the cockpit and get on the loudspeaker and announce my purpose to everyone on the plane! It was one of the most remarkable moments of my life.

Why?

Because when you reveal your true purpose, you have an endless and extraordinary resource for accomplishing great things in any endeavor you choose. It's like you've opened the flood-gates that have been holding back this extraordinary flow of creative energy and it's now rushing into your life.

The power you feel as you get in touch with your purpose is truly incredible. That power is your passion.

PURPOSE = PASSION

Passion, my friends, is the key to your personal power!

Have you ever met, or perhaps seen a movie, or read a book about someone who was passionate about their life? Remarkable, isn't it?

Do you remember Dr. Martin Luther King's speech, "I Have A Dream"? How about President Kennedy's zest for life or his unbelievable assertion that we would put a man on the moon in ten years? Possibly you recall Ghandi's unswerving determination to bring about freedom for his people?

Think about these people for a minute. What is it they have that drives them on to higher and higher levels of accomplishment?

I believe the answer is... passion!

No matter what their individual lifestyle or expression, that bonfire of passion is common to all men and women of greatness. And *purpose* is the driving force that fuels their passion.

Something else shared by all these great, extraordinary people was that their purpose was bigger than life itself.

YOU ARE *EXTRA*-ORDINARY

Remember the movie *Ordinary People?* Well, I believe there's no such thing as ordinary people! I make my living by meeting and working with thousands of so-called ordinary (even by themselves) people every year and I have yet to meet one ordinary person!

Oh, they may be hanging around in some ordinary circumstances for a while. But when they reveal their true purpose and they get a real taste of what's possible for them in their lives, they show me just how extraordinary they really are. I promise you, when someone discovers their real purpose, and you help him or her re-connect with what's really important to them in their lives—*look out!* Their belief system and level of commitment ignite and begin to "blast off"! It's fantastic!

COMMITMENT

And speaking of commitment, let's talk about that right now. Commitment is the biggest "no-big-deal" in our lives. We were born committed. It's true. Commitment isn't something we have to manufacture. It's something within each of us waiting to be discovered. How do we do that? By discovering our purpose.

You see, you cannot commit yourself to anything that isn't aligned with your life's purpose. I would like to share with you the best explanation of commitment, and of the power it can unleash into your life, I've ever read. It was written by W. H. Murray, who was a member of the Second Himalayan Expedition.

Until one is committed there is always hesitancy, the chance to draw back, always ineffectiveness. Concerning all acts of initiative (and creation), there is one elementary truth, the ignorance of which kills countless ideas and splendid plans: that the moment one definitely commits oneself, then Providence moves too. All sorts of things occur to help one that would never otherwise have occurred. A whole stream of events issues from the decision, raising in one's favor all manner of unforeseen incidents and meetings and material assistance, which no man could have dreamt would have come his way.

I have learned a deep respect for one of Goethe's couplets:

Whatever you can do, or dream you can, begin it. Boldness has genius, power, and magic in it."

"Genius, power and magic..." Those are a few neat things to have in your toolbox! Wouldn't you agree? So let's bring them to bear on your goals.

GOALS ARE SMALL STEPS

Now, here's this big, bold vision of truly remarkable proportions (your purpose). How do you begin to bring it about? The answer is one step at a time.

There's an old Chinese saying, "A journey of a thousand miles begins with a single step." That first step, and all the steps that follow, are represented by your goals. Your goals then keep you on track in pursuit of that timeless destination—your purpose. They're also there to help make the trip more rewarding and fun.

GOALS HELP IN MANY WAYS

They help us to get where we're going by measuring our progress. It's like driving to a distant place. First we get to this point on the map, then to this city, to this highway, across this border and so forth. Goals let us know when we're on track and doing well, or when we're off track and need to make an adjustment.

An important point is that they help us build momentum. Each time we accomplish one goal, it gives us more power for the next one, and the next, and so on. When you set a goal...commit to it...hold a vision of it...work toward it and then achieve it...you've really done something. But more important than what you've done is what you've *become*.

What kind of person sets and accomplishes goals?

That's right—*a successful person*.

What kind of person builds a pattern of setting and getting their goals?

Right again—*a successful person*. A person who is building a growing resource of passion to be used in pursuit of their purpose. A powerful person. A person who *empowers* other people.

And I'll give you a little hint about a person's purpose that comes from working with all those extraordinary people—*it always has to do with helping and empowering others!*

BEING ON PURPOSE

Your purpose is a homing beacon that keeps you on track and prevents you from being distracted. Your goals are valuable stepping stones that lead you to *being* your purpose. That's why I say your purpose is unending.

Purpose isn't something you *do*. Purpose is something you *be*. This is a big and very important difference. Living your purpose is *the way you are*. That's *being*. Remember, they call us "human beings," not "human doings."

With a clear, articulated purpose, no matter what comes up in your life, you won't stray. You know which choices serve your purpose and which ones do not.

When times get tough, your purpose can pull you through. Without one, you're unclear as to why you're going through the difficulties.

When your life's purpose is held high and you're down in a valley of despair, you'll always be able to see a glimmer, just over the next hill. So you take your struggles in stride and turn your stumbling blocks into stepping stones. Eventually you climb up and out into the bright light of success.

Your purpose, and the passion that flows from it, is what empowers you to do that—no matter how tough life gets.

WHAT'S SO SPECIAL ABOUT NETWORK MARKETING

It's the perfect place to live the purpose of helping others achieve success in their lives. At the same time, it enables you to make a profound contribution to others. It rewards you personally, financially and in so many other abundant ways—just for *being* who you are.

Not bad for a part-time opportunity!

So, let's talk about things you can *do* to accomplish your goals and how you can *be* the on-purpose person you're aspiring to be through Network Marketing.

YOUR SUCCESSFUL NETWORK MARKETING BUSINESS

First and foremost: take your purpose in one hand and

your Network Marketing opportunity in the other. Now ask yourself this fundamentally important question:

"Is this Network Marketing business of mine, this company, its philosophy and people, these products or this service—the perfect vehicle for me—right now—to assist me in pursuing my life's purpose?"

It's either "yes" or "no." "Maybe" is not the right answer!

It's important to be truthful with yourself in answering this question. If you honestly believe there are faster or better ways for you to get where you want to be—that's great. I suggest you release your business and move on to doing what you really love and want to do. Continue using the products or services if you wish, but it's probably not in your best interest, or the interest of others, to continue as a business. You simply won't do the things necessary to empower yourself or your associates. Can you see the value in discovering this early, before you've invested your time and money?

Now, if you can say "Yes"—*that's great!* That means:

"Yes, this Network Marketing business of mine, this company, these products or services, these people behind this company, this whole concept is the perfect vehicle for pursuing my life's purpose. It will eventually provide the financial resources I need, increase my circle of influence, sharpen my business acumen, and nourish my self-confidence."

If you can say that to yourself, then I say to you... *Why not get passionate about your business?*

Why not recognize it for what it truly is? An opportunity to really express yourself and live your life to the fullest. Quit playing games with it. Make the unconditional commitment to make it work.

If you have only eight hours a week, commit to those eight hours. Do everything you possibly can to make those eight hours as productive as possible. If you have 60 or 80 hours a week to devote to it—then do that!

You might feel you don't know how to do that. Fine. I can help you.

My promise to you is to teach and train you how to use the powerful and proven principles in this book. To mold you into a *master teacher and trainer*. To show you how to use your Network Marketing business so that it helps you accomplish your life's dreams! That's my promise.

Even though it seems a bit outrageous, it's actually an easy one for me to make. Remember, *90 percent of your success is knowing why—and you already know that.* The other 10 percent is *how.* That's what's next.

ESTABLISHING YOUR OWN GOALS

Let's get to a "biggie" right away. Money.

So many people are attracted to Network Marketing "for the money." It's a fact that this business offers fantastic possibilities for generating a phenomenal amount of income, but my friends, *money isn't what it's all about!*

Money literally comes in the wake of you being your purpose.

Let's take the name of my company for instance—

Millionaires In Motion. Sometimes people get the wrong idea about that. The name isn't based on money at all. It's based on my goal of having *one million friends.* It's based on helping people cultivate a "Million Dollar Attitude And Belief System."

I have the greatest respect for our language and the dictionary, but I really think they made a mistake with the word "millionaire." The dictionary says it means someone who has $1,000,000.00 or more in currency. Shouldn't it mean someone who has one million of anything that's valuable? Besides, compare having one million friends with one million dollars. Which would you rather have?

I know many wealthy people in Network Marketing. People earning hundreds of thousands, even a million dollars a year and more. And although some of them were initially attracted to this business for the money, every one of them soon realized that that wasn't what it was all about.

Sometimes the only way to discover that fact is to make all that money and see for yourself. I can hear you now—"Hey, John, that's a lesson I wouldn't mind learning *today!*"

I know, and believe me, you will soon enough. You'll be much happier, much more fulfilled, and much more successful if you can understand this lesson up front. Money can restore some of those "years the locust hath eaten." But not all. Not by a long shot!

LOOK AT THE LEADERS

One thing every leader in Network Marketing knows is

that his or her success is directly dependent upon the success of the men and women in their organization. That's why this is a "Trainer's Training Book." I know that when you become an excellent trainer, you'll be able to teach your entire organization to be successful. And when you do that, the money will simply flow into your life and your bank account.

By the way, here's one useful thing to know about money. It's just a symbol of purchasing power. In and of itself, it can do nothing. So when you work with your goals, don't focus on money. Focus your attention on what you want to *have*, *do*, and *be*.

THE ESSENCE OF GOALS

One sure way to have powerful goals is to discover the essence of those goals.

Just like we did with your purpose, take any goal you have and ask yourself, "When I achieve this, what will it bring me?" And keep asking until you get to the essence. The real bottom line.

Now your goal becomes a powerful picture you can use to represent that essential quality you're after in your life. And I'll tell you, there's no better way to bring a specific goal into your life, than to actively cultivate the essence of what having that goal will bring you. It's a powerful, magnetic force. And I'll give you some great techniques you can use to do that in the next chapter.

One more thing about cultivating the essence of your specific goal.

For the most part, you cannot have your goal right

now—this very moment. Just try to close your eyes and bring a Mercedes into your driveway. You can't do it, can you? *But you can have the essence of that Mercedes—right now!*

Does that Mercedes mean freedom for you, or security? Perhaps having that car means a deep feeling of satisfaction and self-esteem. Well, you can generate all of those feelings *this very moment!* And as I said, having the inner experience of freedom, satisfaction and self-esteem is the best way I know of to create the outward manifestation of that Mercedes or whatever it is you're after.

NOW YOU HAVE THE KEY

Let me be honest with you. The key to this chapter, and for you making this book tremendously successful for yourself, is to tap into the wellspring of your emotions. By being in touch with your true purpose in life and convinced that Network Marketing is aligned with that purpose—you've unlocked your passion. And friend, with your passion flowing, anything is possible!

"Okay, John," you say, "I'm in touch with my purpose. I see how Network Marketing is a great vehicle to enable me to get on with having what I want in my life. But that's now, this very minute. I know it's going to fade some. Maybe a lot. How do I keep it burning? How do I learn what to do to really master this business and be a fantastic success?"

You're so great! I love this. You ask all the right questions. So here we go.

First, turn the page and I'll show you how to take that spark of energy you feel right now, and build it into a *bonfire of passion!* And once you learn that, you'll be able to use that fire to ignite your own life and the lives of literally thousands, perhaps millions of others.

Then, after we've done that, I'll invest the rest of this book giving you a simple, fool-proof, one-step-at-a-time, proven program for mastering Training and Teaching Network Marketing.

Fair enough? Let's go!

Chapter Two:
The Four Fuels

Now, let's take that spark of desire you ignited by getting in touch with your purpose and turn it into a bonfire of passion. We'll do that by adding fuel to the fire so we can make it blaze bigger and brighter than ever before. Specifically, I'm going to give you four forms of fuel for achieving lasting, ongoing success: Visualization, Unshakable Faith, Education and Knowledge, and Your Environment of Support.

W hat is passion *really*?

I say it's having an unshakable faith, a full-blown commitment akin to unconditional love for your life. It's being powerfully in sync with life itself. That's why the source of passion is your life's purpose. Try having that depth of powerful feeling about anything less. It simply doesn't work.

You can feel genuine depth of passion for a loved one, for a project you're involved with, for a sport or hobby. And the truth is that in each of these instances, you're experiencing the unique self-expression of your life's purpose. Passion and purpose are clearly love-and-marriage, a horse-and-carriage kind of relationship.

Passion even *feels* hot. That's why we have such phrases as "… in the heat of passion," or "… building a bonfire of passion." It's powerful stuff!

Passion flows from the very core of your being. And when you've got a clear vision of your life's purpose, when you're experiencing passion and the thing you're doing in your life is a perfect vehicle for expressing that passion—you've got a direct line from the very source of your creative energy right through to this very moment.

Remember the line from the commitment quote, *"Genius, power and magic in it."* That's passion! Wow! What a joy that is!

SO...HOW DO YOU KEEP THE FIRE OF PASSION BURNING?

Another great question. How do you keep any fire burning? You give it fuel.

You know *why* you're in this business. That's your spark of desire. And to that we're going to add four forms of fuel which you're going to use—whenever and wherever you want—to keep that fire going, glowing and building into a bonfire of passion that won't go out... a powerful, purposeful passion for accomplishing all your goals and living your life's purpose to the highest! Here they are:

- Visualization
- Unshakable Faith
- Education and Knowledge
- Your Environment of Support

Let's take them one at a time.

FUEL #1—VISUALIZATION

"A picture is worth a thousand words." You know, I'm not sure that's exactly right. I think a picture is worth a *million words*, maybe more. And it is—if that picture is something you *really* want and you project it powerfully and continuously onto the big movie screen of your mind.

We need to condition our minds to picture the *outcome* of what we want to achieve in life. We need to cultivate our ability to use mental pictures that focus and guide our creative energy to bring what we desire into being.

PICTURES OF FEAR

When I first began in this industry, I had a *terminal fear* of speaking in front of groups. It's true! It's not unusual either. Every time they do a study on people's greatest fears, public speaking is Fear #1. That's amazing, but I truly understand why.

Do you know what fear is?

In its natural state, fear is an instinctive self-protection device. Way back when we were living in caves, fear was the thing that kept us one step ahead of the tiger with the big teeth. That kind of fear was useful then—in fact, it still is. It's the feeling that keeps us from stepping blindly off the curb into the path of an oncoming truck. It's what we sense when we think of war, the consequences that come from abusing our environment, or of acting without integrity, and things like that.

And that "sense" we have comes from pictures we create in our minds.

But there's another set of fear pictures which aren't useful. It's what I call the artificial (rather than natural) kind. And I call it that because it isn't that primal, protecting fear that serves us. It's the self-imposed, fantasy-fear pictures of an uncertain future that limits our life and its possibilities.

Let me tell you a story. While I do, see if you can picture this.

OLD LIONS *CAN* HUNT

Nature fascinates me, and I use a lot of examples from the natural world in my workshops and seminars. One in particular is about lions.

As they age, older lions lose their agility, their power and their teeth as well. They are no longer the fierce predators they once were. But their place in the pride still continues, because their place in the hunt is still of great value.

The pride selects a herd of springboks to attack. The younger, virile lions circle around in one direction while the older lions circle around in the other. When the moment is just right... the old, toothless lions stand up, and feign a charge as they fiercely roar out their presence. The frightened prey, instinctively races off in the opposite direction. Right into the waiting jaws and claws of the pack of hungry young lions.

We people are animals, too. Yet we have been blessed with the ability to discern and distinguish the real dangers of life from the unreal, imagined threats. We are not springboks destined by our ignorance and fear to become a lion's dinner.

We really can do better than that. Yet, all too often, we don't. Why?

Because sometimes, we get crazy.

ARE YOU CRAZY, TOO?

You know, the definition of crazy is someone who isn't in touch with reality. Take the example I just described. Those springbok were crazy. They weren't in touch with reality.

If they had thought for just a moment, they would have realized that a toothless, feeble old lion is no threat to them at all. They would have looked at the old roaring lion, and said, "Are you kidding me?" and bounded away right over his head to safety.

But of course, springboks don't think that way. As far as we know, only people can think like that. Yet we conjure up false fears of an uncertain future all the time. And in truth, we feel *crazy* each time we do that.

Like my fear of speaking in public.

I was fortunate enough, when I began in this business, to have some people around who understood what I was going through. They knew I was "crazy" and they helped me turn my fear into what today is one of my greatest assets. Now I speak to hundreds of people at a time, and I'm able to do it so well, so naturally, effortlessly and effectively, that when I tell people how scared I used to be, they don't believe me! Well, it's true! Here's how I learned what to do.

TURN YOUR FEARS AROUND IN YOUR MIND

I was taught to take time before each presentation to *create a picture in my mind* of the positive result I wanted to achieve.

I began to focus on a picture of a small home meeting... at the end of the meeting, I was standing there and the small group of people who attended were clapping and jumping up to shake my hand, and they were saying, "John, this is fantastic, thank you so much for telling us about this." And they said, "This is amazing. I want to do this business *now*. I really understand what's available for me. This is great! Thanks so much for offering us this chance."

I would walk back and forth before the meeting, just picturing over and over in my mind how much people would get out of the presentation. How empowered they'd be. They would see how they could have all their heartfelt desires by building their own Network Marketing business. I just focused on how great they would feel, on them getting all the benefits possible from that meeting.

I started small—groups of four and five. In a short period of time, I was speaking to bigger and bigger groups of people.

Ten years later, I'm talking to thousands of people around the world—easily, effortlessly—having a ball and getting great results.

I still do the visualization before every single workshop or seminar. Know why? Because even now, after all these successful years, I still get a little crazy sometimes. But now, I just picture people loving every minute of my talk, getting tremendous results, much more than they ever thought possible. And I don't focus on how *I'm* going to do that, just on the results *they* get.

FIVE-YEAR-OLDS PLAYING MOZART

Here's a great story.

In Philadelphia, there's a fairly progressive music school. I believe it's called the New School. They take kids and teach them the most extraordinary things at a remarkably early age. The whole premise is based on the fact that we have a far greater capacity than we ever use, and by starting early with these kids, they'll be able to do extraordinary things. Here's a marvelous example of one of their methods.

They teach the kids to play the violin at four and five years old—and you know what their very first lesson is?

Everybody—kids, parents, teachers, friends—get dressed up in their Sunday best and sit in the school theater. Then one by one, violin and bow in hand, the kids walk up on stage. (Remember now, this is Lesson #1 in learning how to play the violin.) When the kids get to center stage, they bow and the entire audience applauds, cheers, shouts "Bravo! Bravo!" and then the kids walk off and sit down.

That's it. End of their first lesson.

Isn't that great! Imagine the picture that kid is carrying around in his or her mind about playing the violin!

ONE KEY TO VISUALIZATION

Now here's a point that is really interesting to me, which I had not thought of until a friend pointed it out.

I hadn't realized it, but when I visualize the successful outcome of my presentation or meeting—*it's got nothing to do with me!* I'm focused completely on what the people there get out of it. I don't picture "Kalench The Great" and his hundreds of adoring fans. I picture *them*, the people, getting so much benefit they flip out. I see them as being so successful, so inspired—and I think that's an important key!

Just like your life's purpose, visualization is at it's best when it's about *your contribution to others.* It's more powerful if you take your attention off yourself and put it on the other people. That's the real result you want. And you can be sure, when you get that result *for them*— you'll have all *you* desire and more.

Here's what I recommend you do to get into the habit

of picturing the end result. Practice. And one of the best ways I know to do this is Treasure Mapping.

TREASURE MAPPING

A Treasure Map is a collage of pictures that helps stimulate your visualization process. It's made up of pictures of what you want to *do, have* and *be*. A gallery of carefully chosen pictures that represent to you the outcomes you want to create in your life. It contains pictures specifically of those outcomes, and others that strongly suggest the feeling or *essence* of what you want as well.

A Treasure Map can be any size, shape and configuration. You can put it together as one huge poster or book—kind of like a photo album you can pick up and leaf through—or as a series of smaller maps—perhaps one for the car, one for the bathroom mirror, one in your appointment book, and so forth. Your Treasure Map is filled with pictures you cut from a magazine or make yourself.

Here's one of mine.

THE HOUSE ON THE HILL

I live in Southern California, which is one of the most wonderful, beautiful places on Earth. A number of years ago, I would pass this exclusive section of custom built homes every day on my way to and from my office. Boy, were they fantastic, and I dreamed of living in one of those houses.

There was one in particular that I had my eye on. One day, upon learning about Treasure Maps, I mustered the courage to take my camera and drive up to that house. I pulled into the driveway, grabbed my camera, walked up and rang the front door bell. A pleasant woman answered the door, and I said, "Hi, my name is John Kalench. I drive past every morning and evening from my office, and I just love your house. I've just started my own business, and it's going so well that I know I'm going to be able to buy this house in a year or two. This is the place I've always dreamed of. I don't want to impose on you, but I wondered if you would allow me to take a couple of pictures of your house, so that I can look at them every day to help me focus on my dream and accomplish my goal?"

Well, the woman looked at me in an odd sort of way. Then her face broke into a great big smile and she said, "Come in, John, I'd be happy to have you take some pictures. Let me call my husband and we'll both show you around."

They were great. They showed me every part of the house, the fantastic view, just everything. They asked me to sit down, gave me a glass of wine, and we talked for hours about what I did, what they did, about the house and more. What a day!

We took all kinds of pictures. They even took pictures of me sitting in the living room of the house I'd been dreaming of.

As I was leaving, I asked if it would be okay if I called every once in a while to check in with them. They said that would be great. So that's what I did.

I took the pictures to be developed and when they came back, I made a great Treasure Map of "my" house. I looked at it many times each day. It got so that when I closed my eyes, I could picture myself in any and every room of that house. It was wonderful!

In a little over a year, I had the money to buy that house. I called them up and asked if they would be willing to sell it to me. They said no.

I kept in touch month after month, but they still didn't want to sell. They were quite content there, and I certainly knew why. One day, I called to check in with them and they said, "John, you know what? A good friend of ours who lives a couple of houses up the street was here for dinner the other night, and he told us he was thinking of selling his house and moving back East. Let me give you his number. Call and talk to him about it."

That's just what I did. His house was a little higher up the hill, and was of similar construction. It had a beautiful garden, with an even better view. To make a long story short, I made an incredible sweetheart deal with the owner, a great guy who financed the purchase—and I bought that house. Even though it wasn't the exact home I had in my Treasure Map, I was more than satisfied. Besides, I could look down on the house I originally wanted, anytime I wanted. By the way, the owners of that first house became my very good friends.

Isn't that a great story? It's true. Treasure Maps are powerful! Here's another wonderful story.

A TREASURE OF OLYMPIC GOLD

Remember the Olympic Gold Medal Decathalon winner, Bruce Jenner? Well, he'd always been a pretty good athlete, but nobody, least of all himself, spoke of him as a Gold Medal Olympian in the Decathlon. But once he decided to go for it—that was it for Jenner.

He made a big Treasure Map and placed it directly over his bed on the ceiling. On it were pictures of himself winning every one of the ten events in the decathlon— Jenner winning the high jump... Jenner breaking the tape as he crossed the finish line—first again!... Jenner winning the pole vault. Every night before he fell asleep he stared at those pictures. Every morning, the very first thing he'd see when he opened his eyes was himself— Bruce Jenner, Olympic Gold Medalist!

The rest, as they say, is history.

You can make a Treasure Map just as powerful and just as personal as I did for my "House on the Hill," or as Bruce Jenner did for his Gold Medal.

Let's say you want a new car. Okay, get your camera, grab the family, and troop on down to the dealer's showroom. Have the salesperson help you establish precisely the car you want: make, model, color, everything and have him or her locate that car on the lot. Then you and the family climb in as the salesperson takes a couple of pictures for you—in *your* car. Go to another dealership, if you have to, to find the exact car you want. When you're done, thank the salesperson, mention the date you'll be back to pick it up, and go take your film to be processed.

When you get the prints back, put one or two on your Treasure Map along with all your other pictures. Every day, a number of times each day, look at your Treasure Map. It's filled with images that stimulate you, that remind you of all you want to accomplish. And what's more, all the words and pictures on it are about a done deal. They're not about things off in the future *someday*. There you are, driving that car *now*, taking that trip *now*, having, using, enjoying whatever it is you want—*now*.

USE YOUR TREASURE MAP FOR BOTH YOUR GOALS AND YOUR PURPOSE

Your Treasure Map isn't just for the things you want. You can use it for what you want to *be* as well. It's perfect for envisioning yourself building that highly successful Network Organization.

At your next company meeting, have a picture taken with the upline leaders in your organization. Have one taken with the company president shaking your hand. Clip pictures out of magazines of people making successful presentations, or speaking to large groups of people. Don't forget words, either. You can cut out headlines or words that really speak to you. Words like, "She's great" or "The Great American Success Story."

The whole point of your Treasure Map is to give your mind picture after picture of you as an accomplished success. Your mind will take these pictures and absorb them right down into your subconscious as an accomplished fact.

Look—your mind doesn't distinguish between what's real or imagined. If you don't believe me, try this.

Close your eyes, relax and have a friend or family member describe point-by-point, in the most vivid detail, you standing with the tips of your shoes over the edge of the roof of the World Trade Center in New York City! That's 110 stories above the street!

Keep at it until you actually feel the wind gusting around you and *keep looking down*—all 100-plus dizzy stories down at the tiny cars and the ant-sized people. How do you feel? Safe and secure? I'll bet. Your subconscious didn't wait for a moment to see if this was *real* or not. It jumped to your rescue instantly, didn't it?

You can use that same subconscious power to do things other than scare the heck out of yourself. Can you see how amazing this is?

That's the power of a Treasure Map. And believe me, even if you've had years of self-doubt about what you could do in your life, it doesn't take long for that Treasure Map and those pictures to start weighing down the scales in your mind on the "I Can" side. And once those scales tip in your favor—you just have to keep showing up to get what you want.

So I encourage you now to list and then prioritize the goals—the stepping stones—the forms of acknowledgement—you wish to bring into your life as a result of your business.

Within the next 12 months, what do you see yourself *Having—Becoming—and Doing* as a result of this wonderful vehicle—your Networking business? List everything that comes to your mind—then go back and choose the five most important ones. Please do this exercise now!

Within the next 12 months, I...

_____

_____

_____

_____

_____

_____

Within the next three to five years, what do you see yourself *Having—Becoming—and Doing* as a result of your new business opportunity? Again, list everything that comes to your mind—then go back and choose the five most important ones. Please do this exercise now!

Within the next three to five years, I...

_____

_____

_____

_____

_____

_____

It is these, your ten most important goals for the next one to five years, that I strongly suggest you build your Treasure Map upon. And if you can visualize a picture of it—don't forget to include your "life's purpose" in your Treasure Map. Do this and you'll begin to instill within yourself the kind of passion that will make you unstoppable. The kind of passion where everyone will want to be around you, because they love your heat!

FUEL #2—UNSHAKABLE FAITH

Have you ever wondered why people in Network Marketing usually say "You've gotta love your product?" Because when you go out and start talking to people about the benefits of your product and your opportunity, you're bound to hear a "No thanks, I'm not interested." You may even hear a number of them.

If you're unsure that your product *really* gets the results you say, if you doubt that this business is *really* simple and fun, that you can make money, and that the people who sponsored you *really* will help you build it successfully—what do you think will happen? A couple of "no's" and you're a goner.

You've got to be able to hear "No" and say to yourself, "I know my product is worth it, and I know my opportunity is worth it. It must be that it's just not the right time for them." Say thanks—and move on. That's having unshakable faith.

How do you develop unshakable faith? Here's one key.

I want you to tattoo on the inside of your forehead the following big, bold, block letters:

SW, SW, SW—NEXT

They stand for: Some Will, Some Won't, So What—*Next!*

In Network Marketing, you do not convince... you do not persuade with charm nor manipulate with cleverness.

Network Marketing is the "sorting" business. You have faith in your company and your product based on your own *experience*, and then you make your offer. You recommend your product or service to others. And *some will* say yes, and *some won't*, and *so what*—who's *next?*

This business is all about sharing the *right thing*, with the *right people*, at the *right time*.

Nothing else will help you develop the foundation you need to succeed in Network Marketing like having unshakable faith. "Great," you say, "and just how do I get *that?*" Thanks for asking. The answer is...

WHOM DO YOU TRUST?

You may be old enough to remember how the *Tonight Show*'s Johnny Carson started in television. He did an afternoon TV quiz show with Ed McMahon called "Who Do You Trust?" That's the important question you've got to ask yourself. Because when it comes right down to it, there's only one person who matters where trust is concerned. That's right—you know who.

THE GUY IN THE GLASS

I have a dear friend who was struggling in his business for some time. He's a great guy, yet he was experiencing all sorts of difficulties.

His friends at times, weren't supportive. He'd gotten involved with the wrong opportunity in the beginning, and some important people in his life were trying to influence him to get out of this business. But he loves people and Network Marketing—and he's great at it, too. He really believes in himself and he knows it's just a question of time and the right vehicle (opportunity), before he succeeds.

The other night I attended a function where he was. All night long he kept looking in his organizer. I was really curious, so after the meeting I went over and asked him, "Why do you keep opening your notebook?"

He said that there was a poem he had placed in his notebook, and that whenever he gets a little discouraged and starts to question himself and have doubts, he reads this poem.

When he read it to me, it touched me deeply. It's called *The Guy In The Glass*. Here it is.

When you get what you want in your struggle for self,
And the world makes you king for a day,
Then go to the mirror and look at yourself,
And see what that guy has to say.
For it isn't your mother, your father, or wife
Whose judgment on you you must pass.
The fellow whose verdict counts most in your life,
Is the guy staring back from the glass.
He's the fellow to please, never mind all the rest,
For he's with you clear to the end.
And you've passed your most dangerous and difficult test,
If the guy in the glass is your friend.

You may be like Jack Horner and chisel a plum,
And think you're a wonderful guy,
But the guy in the glass says you are a bum,
If you can't look him straight in the eye.
You may fool the whole world down the pathway of years
And get pats on the back as you pass,
But the final reward will be heartache and tears
If you've cheated the guy in the glass.

Anonymous

Now, it's in my organizer as well.

CONFIDENCE COMES FROM COMPETENCE

You've got to develop *confidence* in yourself. The word "confidence" comes from two words which literally mean *trust by heart*. Isn't that great! So, you either *trust by heart* this business, your product and opportunity—or you don't. Nobody can do it for you. Confidence comes from within you.

Use the products. Experience how well they work. Go to every meeting, every Opportunity Showcase and company function you can possibly get to. Because when you do, you'll continuously be exposed to men and women having direct experiences of success with both your product and your opportunity.

This can be a big help to you in the beginning. Do it. It works.

Do you know why I insist that training is so very important? Because a well-trained person is a competent, confident person. He or she knows what to do and when to do it.

You could get lucky. You could be the one-in-a-million who was born to it. But if you're like me, and millions of others, it's going to take training and practice—and with that, I promise you will be competent. The training part is my responsibility. The practice part is yours.

I'm serious. I know you'll begin to notice there's good stuff here, but you won't really get to the secret until you're all the way through. Then it'll probably hit you like a bolt of lightning. "Wow. Yeah. It's all coming together. This is great!"

FUEL #3—EDUCATION AND KNOWLEDGE

This is so very important!

There are people who have gone where you want to go and are willing to share with you all they know about what got them there. You only have to be open to receiving their wisdom. Reinventing the wheel is anti-Network Marketing.

I would like to right now acknowledge you for being in the top 20 percent of the people in this business. You think enough of yourself, enough of your dreams, and enough of your business to invest both your time and money in pursuing the knowledge that's in this book.

You know, and this really amazes me, a lot of people think knowledge is expensive. There are people who think the price of this book is expensive!

I suppose these are the same people who will spend an average of $600 a year on the *outside* of their heads—haircuts, sprays, hair dryer, hats, you name it—and squawk when you suggest they invest $100 for a workshop or home study course—or $12.95 for a book. For those people who think education and knowledge is expensive, I say, "You're not taking a hard enough look at the cost of ignorance!"

One idea alone, from an educational book, magazine or workshop, can make you thousands, even tens of thousands of dollars or more. I have an associate who took an idea he got from a business newsletter (for which he paid over $100 a year) and sold it to a client one week after he read it for a $7000 profit! Knowledge is power—money power especially!

Benjamin Franklin said it so well:

Take everything that you own and put it in your mind. That way nobody can steal it.

Our mind is what separates us from the rest of the animals. Continue to invest in your mind. I guarantee the return is phenomenal.

So, I acknowledge you for being a special person. And I promise you, your openness and willingness will generate great success for you. It's only a matter of time—and a very short time at that!

FUEL #4—YOUR ENVIRONMENT OF SUPPORT

If you were a *phenomenal success* in your Network Marketing business... if you became one of the top ten producers in the entire world with your company... if you were a leader of leaders, Distributor of the Year, a man or woman who was called upon to be an inspiration to all the people in the company, the community, and yes, even throughout the world... would your life be any different than it is now?

Of course it would.

I'm not talking about humility, or whether or not you'd forget your old friends because you were suddenly a mega-success. I'm talking about where you'd be, what you'd be doing, who you'd "hang out" with. All that would change for you, and probably quite dramatically, too.

So? So... why not make some of those changes—*now*? I'm not talking about "fake it 'til you make it." I'm not suggesting that you run your credit cards up to the max to carry on the illusion of success. I'm talking about using your environment as an external stimulus to help you bring into being all that you truly desire.

Have you ever heard the advice, "If you want to be a success, hang around with successful people?" Here's a more down-home way of saying the same thing:

It's impossible to fly like an eagle, if you only surround yourself with turkeys.

I'm not telling you to give up your ol' beer drinkin' buddies or call a halt to that precious Monday morning "get together over coffee" with the girls. What I am suggesting is that you arrange your environment so that every single aspect of it contributes to your achieving higher and higher levels of personal and professional success.

Certainly, Treasure Maps, Unshakable Faith in your product or service and your company, and a commitment to your continued Education and Knowledge are part of your environment. And there's more.

SURROUND YOURSELF WITH SUCCESS

You know one thing I've discovered about successful people? They immerse themselves in excellence. Oh, they still have their delightful idiosyncrasies. I know a top corporate, Fortune 500 CEO who insists on eating sandwiches that are uncut, the whole two-fisted handful, and having his beer from a can, while eating off $260 plates in the executive dining room. And he may also get a kick out of watching "Wrestle Mania" on his TV, too. That's not what I mean.

What I mean is that you *seek out excellence* in all that you do, in all that you say, in all that you are. Tom Peters said it best in his second best-selling book—in fact, he said it simply in the book's title: *A Passion For Excellence.* That's what I'm talking about.

You want to surround yourself with men and women who share common minds, common goals and common purpose with you. You want to stand apart from the crowd, march to the beat of Thoreau's "different drummer," dare to be great.

Read great books, see fine films, eat good food, do all those things that you can afford to do that keep you in the company of greatness.

Seek out those men and women in your company who are acknowledged leaders. Learn from them. If you can "hang out" with them—*do it!* Look, this isn't "being too big for your britches." This is being smart.

WHOM DO YOU FOLLOW?

I believe it's very smart for each person who's striving to become the best he or she can be in whatever they do to have role models of excellence to follow. To choose carefully the qualities and individuals they respect and admire the most. And identify these mentors as shining examples to follow and mirror.

I personally have a number of mentors. One of whom is my father. Not because of his entrepreneurial example, but rather because of his unconditional love he continually displays for my mother—his wife. I've never met a man who is so open and proud in showering his affection for the number one person in his life. I can't tell you how this makes me feel everytime I see them. I can tell you, I want to create that same kind of love in my life. So my father, (my mentor), is my life's reminder, my hero, the shining example I try to follow! Who are your mentors?

LOOKING GREAT

Dress for success. Show up for your meetings in a suit and tie or your sharpest dress. Look professional and successful and you'll feel the same. Join the industry trade organization—the Multi-level Marketing International Association (MLMIA). Subscribe to the finest publications in the industry. Read the best books. Listen to the best tapes. Surround yourself with positive, high-energy, successful people.

Don't participate in negative talk—even under the

heading of "being realistic." Seek out and cultivate high quality and success in everything you do, and say, and associate with. It *will* rub off.

I know these four forms of fuel will transform your spark of desire into a bonfire of passion for success! They have worked for me and countless others since man first decided to learn, to grow and to *be* more. Here they are once again:

Fuel #1—Visualization
Fuel #2—Unshakable Faith
Fuel #3—Education and Knowledge
Fuel #4—Your Environment Of Support

Do you see how these four forms of fuel can feed you daily? Do you see how you can tap into your passion at any time and fuel it to blaze bigger and brighter than ever before? And do you see that you can do this at any moment you choose?

These four fuels are an extraordinary resource of power for you. And each of them is always available, because they come from *within* you!

THERE YOU HAVE IT!

Well, what else is there? Now, you know it all. Get out there and set the world on fire!

What? Just one more little thing…?

What's that?

Oh—you want to know "*How*"?

I'll bet you're one of those people who's from Missouri.

You know, the kind who likes to challenge guys like me with, "Oh yeah, show me."

All right, my friend. That's just what I'm going to do. And I promise, the remainder of this book will show you *how*.

I've told you that knowing *why* is 90 percent of the game, and you may ask, "Then why is 90 percent of this book about *how*?" That's a great question. And you know what, I'm not sure why that is.

But I am sure about this. When you've finished this book, and you read it again, and a third time as well, immediately start putting into practice what you learn. Get out there and train your people with these principles and techniques. If you just do that and you have even the slightest doubt that this book is worth *ten times the price you paid for it*, you write me and tell me that, and I will send you my personal check for the full cost you paid. No questions asked. Is that fair enough?

The guy in the glass wouldn't have it any other way.

You see, I have Unshakable Faith in what I'm teaching you *and* in your success. And when you finish this book, you will too.

IMPORTANT NOTE:

I know that many of you will have not completed the "Purpose and Goals" exercises while reading the book for the first time. I know this because I would do the same thing—thinking that I would complete them when I finished reading the entire chapter or book!

Please, if that's what you've done, go back and do the exercises right now. It's so very important for you to understand *why* you are doing this business before you learn *how*. It is the foundation upon which this book is built. And your future success in Network Marketing depends on it.

I also suggest that you do the exercises in pencil. As you grow both personally and professionally, you may want to change things—and make them better and better. And remember, think BIG—*Boldness has genius, power and magic in it!*

Chapter Three:
Training: Your First Step

Training is the foundation upon which you build your success in this business. As I've said before, the fastest, most powerful way to master a subject is to teach it to others. When you understand why training is so important and how to begin your own training program, you'll take the first giant step in building a growing, enduring, successful Network Marketing business of your own, and you'll be well on your way to creating true financial freedom.

There are basically two kinds of people who come into Network Marketing.

I like to refer to the first group as the Al and Alice Achievers. They're people who understand that there are proven principles for doing anything successfully. They know that if they're able to learn from the experts by mirroring and modeling the experts' accomplishments, it's very likely that they will achieve the same degree of success—if not greater. Al and Alice are the kind of people who go out of their way to acquire that knowledge.

Sometimes there are training programs provided by their company or their upline, and Al and Alice pursue these with a passion. All they're after is just two or three little "Ah-Ha's" that they know can change the total outcome of their business.

Other times, they're not fortunate enough to have specific training programs or even sponsors who will provide this needed education. But the Achievers go out and get that knowledge anyway. They don't try to re-invent the wheel. They discover, on their own if need be, what those processes, those success principles are. They'll get it through other people, through training programs or through educational tools, such as books or tapes.

Now, the Al and Alice Achievers represent about 20 percent of the people in our industry. The other 80 percent, I refer to as the Herman and Hillary Hope-It-Happens.

CUTTING THROUGH THE B.S.

The fundamental difference between these two couples is their attitude.

Al and Alice honestly believe—with all their hearts and minds and with their entire beings—that they *deserve* to be prosperous and successful.

Herman and Hillary Hope-It-Happens are not at that point yet. Their self-esteem is very low. Maybe they've experienced a number of failures in their lives; consequently, they believe that success can't *really* happen for them.

Herman and Hillary have built a habit of negative thinking which perpetuates failure. They rarely focus on the main ingredient of success—*the belief that they can be successful!* So what they really have to work on first is cutting through their B.S.—their *Belief Systems.*

BELIEF SYSTEMS THAT WORK

There's some conventional wisdom that says belief systems in general are wrong and they don't work. I disagree. I say that belief systems *that don't work* are wrong.

Al and Alice Achiever have a belief system that tells them they're going to succeed. Now, that's a belief system that supports and empowers them!

The Hope-It-Happens, on the other hand, have a dysfunctional belief system. It limits their possibilities for the future. All they've got is the *Hope* that someday *It* will *Happen.* They don't really think they have a chance— and truthfully, with that belief system in place, they don't.

Network Marketing makes it easy for people to get started in a business of their own with little or no risk at all. At the same time, it paints such a fantastic picture of the possibilities—both real and imagined—it attracts a lot of Hermans and Hillarys.

Consequently, they usually jump from opportunity to opportunity *hoping that the next* one is somehow, magically, going to do it for them. They actually think they'll achieve success if they can just find "the perfect product" or "get in early enough" with "the right opportunity."

Certainly, aligning yourself with a product and a company that you believe in passionately—is essential! But success doesn't come from the outside. It comes from within. As Anton Chekhov said, *"Man is what he believes."*

TRAINING BEGINS WITH YOUR BELIEFS

What's the biggest challenge you face in building a large, successful Network Marketing business?

You know, most people think it's learning everything there is to know about marketing the product and teaching that knowledge to others... or that it's being able to master the business-building principles and show all your people how to duplicate what you've done... or being a great sales person or a dynamic leader. But it's not any one of these.

The biggest challenge you face in building a large, successful business, is to constantly look at new ways of shifting the belief systems and raising the self-esteem of the people you associate with. And that starts with *yourself.*

BE AN INSPIRATION

When I first started in this business, one of my goals was to become a powerful motivator. Well, I became one—and you know what? Motivation isn't it.

Now my goal is to *inspire* people. The difference between the two is that motivation is only temporary. That's because it's an outside stimulus. *Inspiration* is very different.

When you inspire people, you turn on a light *within* them. You help them see their real potential. Motivation can excite people, but it doesn't last—because it doesn't always fit into their existing belief systems.

You can motivate people with fantastic success stories and get them really pumped up, but if they believe they don't deserve success, or that they don't have what it takes—forget it. Information like that is great, but it's only the form—in*form*. It lives outside the person.

Inspiration is—in*spirit*. It comes from within. It's the difference between giving someone a fish or teaching them how to fish. When you inspire people you change their belief systems—and you help them change their lives!

The foundation of a successful Network Marketing business, which your training program must accomplish *first*, is to set up the belief system of success.

AGAIN AND AGAIN AND AGAIN

Repetition is like the steady dripping of water on a stone. Through the ages, it does make an indentation. Throughout this book, I'm going to mention a number of key points again and again. I'm being "redundantly redundant" for a good reason. Simply because these key issues are very important!

So I'm going to say them again and again (as I said!) And that in itself is an important aspect of every training program. Don't be afraid to repeat, and repeat, and repeat again and again the points that truly are fundamental. That's the best way to make sure your people really understand those points and make them their own.

Here's the first point I'll be returning to throughout the book.

THE MOST COMMON MISTAKE IN TRAINING

Here's what I think is a big mistake most people make when it comes to Network Marketing training: *the people doing the training are usually the most seasoned, successful distributors.*

Now, when you reflect upon that, you'll notice that those seasoned distributors have been in the business for at least six months to a year, if not more. During that time they have acquired a tremendous amount of knowledge about the product, about the company, about the marketing plan, about the whole business opportunity and about all the principles of building a successful Network Marketing enterprise.

It's completely natural, but we forget how long it took us to learn all of that. Then we take some brand new distributors and immediately try to catch them up to us— *within the first couple of hours.* It's crazy!

Even if our new people get all excited about the possibilities temporarily, what we end up doing is creating a belief system in their mind that says, "Overload." They simply cannot imagine themselves comprehending what we've told them. We shove so much information down their throats all at one time, we can't help but confuse even the brightest and most willing of people!

Have you ever explained your Compensation Plan to someone who got it all the first time! It's all very confusing. And when people get confused, it's a natural reaction to think, "I just can't do this. Maybe this really isn't for me."

THINK ABOUT IT

If you've been around awhile, reflect back to some of those new people you thought were really excited about your opportunity. Then, once they learned more about what it was going to take, you didn't hear from them anymore. Or, you heard a number of excuses as to why they couldn't do it.

Well think about it! Is it possible that they heard too much about the *how to's* before they discovered the *whys*? Is it possible they were not yet connected closely enough to the right reasons before they were taught the system and method?

Now, if they were unquestionably clear as to *why* this opportunity was so important to them and their future— maybe, just maybe, their belief system would have been strong enough to withstand those early periods of doubt, fear and rejection.

ONE STEP AT A TIME

The point I'm building to is this: I believe training should be done in stages, and that new people coming into the business should go through a New Distributor Training program that is short and sweet. And that the things they need to discover and learn first—are taught first!

Its objective is to accomplish a few specific things, but not to give new people that whole mountain of information—most of which is totally unnecessary for them to have before they go out and start building their own businesses.

At this point, I'm not going to give you the precise format for your training program. In Chapter Ten, "New Distributor Training," I'll show you where and when this training takes place and just how to do it.

For now, and all the way through the rest of the book until you get to Chapter Ten, I just want you to understand the individual parts of the entire training process. You'll see how it all comes together soon enough.

By the way, if you can't resist putting these ideas into practice immediately—that's great. However, I strongly suggest that you *read the whole book at least three times* before you begin to train your people with these ideas.

A FOUNDATION OF ENTHUSIASM

No matter what your product, service or company, every Network Marketer is in the *Enthusiasm* business.

The most successful men and women in our business

are those who can share their enthusiasm naturally and effortlessly with others. We call it "transferring enthusiasm."

The best way you can help people transfer their enthusiasm is when they understand, as clearly as possible, that what they have to offer is really great!

In other words, when they first make the decision to start sharing the product and the opportunity with other people, they already have a certain degree of enthusiasm within them. Now what we want to do is simply help them become more effective in *transferring* that enthusiasm to others. That's what the New Distributor Training is really for.

I'm not talking about becoming product experts or business opportunity experts, but to help people become more effective in *giving away* their enthusiasm about the products and the business opportunity.

Enthusiasm is a wonderful commodity. It actually has the wonderful capacity to expand and grow in direct proportion to the amount you give to others!

No matter how much enthusiasm you give away, you always have more. That's because enthusiasm doesn't come from outside you. It comes from within.

Now this is interesting. Enthusiasm is made up of two Greek words: *Enthos*, which means "within," and *Theos*, which means "God" or "spirit." So enthusiasm actually means "spirit or God within." You've seen truly enthusiastic people—don't they embody that definition?

WHERE DOES ENTHUSIASM COME FROM?

It's a product of our passion.

That's why I started this book with an introduction about this wonderful Network Marketing business—what a gift it is, how powerful and compelling it is. When you understand and love this industry, do you think you'll be able to transfer your enthusiasm about it? You bet!

It's also why the first chapter is about Your Goals and Purpose. When people are connected with their purpose and they see that Network Marketing is the perfect vehicle for them to experience and express that purpose in their lives—enthusiasm pours out of them naturally and effortlessly.

That's why making the connection with your purpose is so powerful. And when we use the Four Forms of Fuel to feed the passion of our purpose—anytime we need or want to—we become unstoppable!

I highly recommend that you have all your new distributors read "Your Introduction" and the first two chapters of this book before they come to your New Distributor Training program. That way, you won't have to cut through any dysfunctional belief systems they may have.

They'll know *why* they're there and *why* they want to succeed. You won't have to teach them how to generate enthusiasm. Your job will simply be to channel their existing power of creative passion and energy in the right direction.

Simply put, they'll already know where they're going—you'll simply be there to show them the way.

IASM

A key to the word enthusiasm is in the last four letters: I A S M. They stand for "I Am Sold Myself."

Besides being "sold" on themselves and on the industry, there are two basic things about which you can help your new distributors be "sold."

Number one is *the product*.

Number two is *the opportunity*.

In your New Distributor Training program, there should be basic product knowledge and basic business knowledge—but you've got to keep it very, very basic.

A NEW DISTRIBUTOR NEEDS *NEW* DISTRIBUTOR TRAINING

Once again, I believe in a new distributor going through a *New* Distributor Training program. Not a new distributor going through a training program that's being put on by someone who's been in the business for two years.

It's no good if the first thing a new distributor is exposed to is all the specialized information about the product, or how the second half of the marketing plan works and all this other complicated, detailed, technical stuff. They'll learn that in good time—later.

I believe a New Distributor Training program should be conducted by a relatively new distributor, one who is experiencing great success. You want someone who's fairly new to the business. A person with good energy.

And why is that so important?

Because Network Marketing is driven by *duplication*.

A brand new distributor trying to duplicate a seasoned pro who's been in the business for years and is making $50,000 a month is tough. Most of the new people take one look at that—and their hearts sink! Simply because, at this point, they can't imagine themselves being *that* successful.

You want your trainer to be a model that's *actually possible for anyone to duplicate*. And that person just walks these new distributors through the two basic facets of the business: number one is products—some *basic* product knowledge—and number two is some *basic* business knowledge.

Now, I'm not saying there is no place for the seasoned, successful Network Marketers. Far from it. Besides being a real and present inspiration, these men and women are the richest resources in your Network. They've all "been there before." They make superb coaches. They are perfect for the advanced training of leadership skills, because they are the leaders.

What I'm pointing out is that in the beginning, you should have newer people conduct your New Distributor Training. This is so for two reasons: First, they are "reachable" role and goal models. Second—and this will become more and more clear throughout the book—you want your new distributors *themselves* to be teaching the training process as soon as possible. Remember, my premise is: *you master Network Marketing by teaching Network Marketing to others.* The sooner you and your people start training others—the better.

And don't think for a moment that it takes months and months to train a good trainer. With the system I'll show you in this book, you can have your new distributors training other people in two to three weeks!

Before we look at all the individual elements of your New Distributor Training program, let's talk about one more thing.

BEYOND "EARN WHILE YOU LEARN"

Network Marketing is a system where you can earn while you learn. Unlike other professions that require years of education for which you pay, in Network Marketing you learn by doing—and *it pays you!*

That's a pretty revolutionary approach. However, let's take it one very profound and powerful step farther.

Not only will you earn while you learn, but you will learn faster and more powerfully—which will have a direct impact on your earning power as well—*by teaching what you're learning to others.*

We put a great deal of emphasis today on teaching our children. As a parent, your job is to help your kids learn right and wrong, to acquire sound values and develop strong character. But you know what? Ask any parent: who really learns the most in the relationship, you or your children?

Clearly, we learn much more by teaching.

And there is nothing more powerful than teaching what you're learning, if for no other reason than this: *while you are learning, you are wide open to all the possibilities. You hunger to master your subject, to explore new and better ways to understand it, to do it.* The Zen masters call this "beginner's mind." It's a fundamental aspect of my approach.

The New Distributor Training program you'll be learning in this book is so easily duplicatable that you will be able to master the principles and share them effectively with others in a matter of hours and weeks.

Think for a moment: what do you already know about connecting with your purpose and fueling your passion?

When you read those first two chapters again, and then read them one more time and begin to apply the principles in your life and business, do you think you can show other people how to reconnect with their purpose?

Could you teach someone how to use the Four Forms of Fuel? To create a Treasure Map? How about the importance of Education and Knowledge or having Unshakable Faith? Once you've read and understand them by doing them yourself—yes, you can teach others to do the same!

I know you can accomplish all of that and more, because I've watched countless people do that very same thing. That's the remarkable power of this unique training system. It simply harnesses your natural abilities to learn and share what we've learned with others.

Please understand, this isn't about being perfect, either. It's about being on the path of Mastery in Network Marketing. And you are already far down the road on that journey.

Here's what's next: An overview of my entire teaching system. That's what the rest of this book is all about.

THE ELEMENTS OF YOUR
NEW DISTRIBUTOR TRAINING

CHAPTER 4: THE PRODUCTS

Loving your product or service. Becoming a Master of Benefits. Having all the answers (or knowing how to get them). Knowing who's your best customer. Learning how to share your enthusiasm so naturally and so powerfully, most people will find it (and you) irresistible!

CHAPTER 5: PROSPECTING

Getting out of the convincing business and into the sorting business. Working smart (not just hard). Establishing Priorities. Making the entire world your oyster. Plus powerful ways to use the telephone, both local and long distance, and much more.

CHAPTER 6: PRESENTATIONS

K I S & D—Keeping It Simple and Duplicatable. It's not so much what you say, but how you say it. Better yet, how you get your prospect to say it! The power of a Presentation Book. Helping your prospects make the right choice—time after time after time.

CHAPTER 7: OBJECTIONS

Ninety percent of objections are common—they're asked and answered all the time. When you learn them, they quickly become opportunities in work clothes. Learn how you can be a detective. How to listen for and answer your prospect's underlying questions and how to turn these stumbling blocks into stepping stones.

CHAPTER 8: FOLLOW UP AND FOLLOW THROUGH

Customer Service and Satisfaction is where it's at. Building your "business in a box" enables you to be effortlessly organized and amazingly productive. How you can get outstanding results by being a master story teller—your key to power and success.

CHAPTER 9: OPPORTUNITY MEETINGS AND SHOWCASES

Meetings can be fun and fresh, effective and inspiring, simple and duplicatable—and they can cause explosive momentum and growth for your Network. The five key questions in this chapter are worth a fortune!

CHAPTER 10: NEW DISTRIBUTOR TRAINING

Teaching your children well. Preparing them for the real world. Here's "where the rubber meets the road"—where it all comes together. In this chapter, you'll take a step-by-step look at the entire training system—and your business will become supercharged!

CHAPTER 11: DUPLICATION

Your baby eagles were meant to soar! Here's what to do within the first two days, two weeks and two months of their birth. When you grasp these principles and put them into practice, your success and financial freedom become inevitable!

There you have it. That's what you have to look forward to. I hope these next few hours will be the most revealing, exciting and productive of your life.

What you hold in your hands is the key to success in this business. People have been searching for this for years. Does that sound arrogant? It's not. Arrogance is unwarranted self-importance. That's not what I'm saying. What I'm saying is:

One: *You hold the key in your hands*—its got nothing to do with me. Without you, these proven principles and practices mean nothing.

Two: *What you are learning works!* And to prove that, all you have to do is to begin to apply these principles. Just pick one and try it out. You will see immediately and directly experience for yourself, how powerful and right on they are.

Are you ready for extraordinary success? Great! Let's move on. The next chapter is about—The Products!

Chapter Four:
The Products

In Network Marketing, the product or service you're offering is King and Queen. As I've said a number of times already, you've got to be your own best customer. Because our business is built upon sharing and sorting (rather than convincing), there is nothing that can take the place of your loving your product. You can experience love for your product in one of two ways: either love at first sight, or you can learn to love it. In this chapter, we'll look at ways for you to have the best of both worlds.

Have you ever been in the company of someone who deeply and passionately loved something— a person who loves baseball, or art, or music, or anything at all? Boy, they are one of the most powerful forces in the world!

Why? We've discussed a number of the reasons already: purpose... passion... enthusiasm... People alive with these qualities are irresistible.

You may not care about batting averages or who's the greatest shortstop the game has ever known, but you can easily be swept up and away in the sheer devotion and joy that the baseball fan feels for the sport.

"Everybody loves a lover," the song says, and it's true. When someone is in love with something or someone, those powerful feelings are extremely contagious.

Now, imagine for a moment that a friend of yours has recently discovered a product that has changed her life. The last time you saw her was nothing compared to seeing her now. She looks ten years younger! She's got great color and energy. She's just bursting with happiness and life!

"What's happened?" you ask. And she begins to tell you.

A "LABOR" OF LOVE

"John, I just can't believe it! I'm so excited I'm going to burst if I don't share this with you.

"Remember how I was always on some exotic diet?— constantly trying this one or that, yet even if I did lose weight, I couldn't keep it off. My clothes didn't fit. I looked and felt just awful.

"Well all that has changed! I lost 20 pounds in just three weeks—and that was three months ago! It's still off! I weigh less now than I did back in college! I'm seldom hungry because I'm eating all the great tasting foods I want! And I look and feel fantastic! What do you think? Don't I look great!

"And you know what, John—it hasn't cost me a penny. In fact, last month, they paid me $600! Do you know what I do? I just talk to people like you. That's all! And I'm earning enough money to buy my new car! Come take a look at this!"

Boring isn't it? No enthusiasm there. Another poor gal just gettin' by.

You know, I meet so many people with this overflowing, rich, contagious enthusiasm for their products and services, that I have a house full of Network Marketing products! I simply cannot resist someone who's so excited, so in love with his or her products. These people are totally wonderful! They're so full of life and love. Network Marketing truly is "A Labor of Love."

A CHINESE PROVERB

I've always been fascinated by Eastern philosophy, especially the wisdom of China.

The Chinese have a saying that goes something like this: When someone shares with you something of value, and you derive benefit from it, you have an obligation to share it with others.

The Chinese feel it is our responsibility to give to others what has been given to us. It's kind of like guaranteeing that the constant flow of good things that comes around continues to go around. I think this is a beautiful insight into our Network Marketing process of sharing.

When you have received the benefits of a product or service, and you in your turn share that product with others, you are fulfilling a natural obligation. By the way, the Chinese alphabet is made up of word-pictures, and the one for obligation also means "the road back to your home." Isn't that interesting?

In "Your Introduction," I mentioned that Network Marketing was a system that, in my opinion, mirrors the natural order of things. It seems so right for us to share what we've been given. Just as right as it is to be rewarded for doing so.

I guess you could say that learning about a wonderful product or service and *not* sharing it with others is selfish. At any rate, I enjoy thinking that when we share our products with people we are really making a contribution to others—giving in return for what we've been given.

PRODUCT VERSUS OPPORTUNITY

There are some schools of thought that say it's the opportunity that attracts people to this business, and that's the real value of Network Marketing.

I flatly disagree.

Without a superb product you would have no Network Marketing business.

The most lucrative compensation plan in the world will not provide you an on-going income, if the product or service doesn't provide tangible value and benefits for your customers. It's been proven time and time again.

Some Network Marketing companies in the past have tried to offer fantastic opportunities and mediocre products. And some of them have even started off with impressive initial sales—but they seldom last. That's because the marketplace is the final judge and jury.

P. T. Barnum said, "There's a sucker born every minute." At the current birth rate levels, that puts suckers in the smallest of minorities. No, people are not stupid. Far from it. More and more, the consumer demands the highest quality performance from the goods and services he or she purchases.

In Network Marketing you earn money on the sales of products or services *only*. Poor products—poor earnings. The business opportunity is the reward structure that supports you and compensates you directly for your efforts. *There is no lasting value without a strong product or service.*

LIFE-ENHANCING AND LIFE-CHANGING PRODUCTS

Whether you're dealing with nutritional or diet products, financial services, discount phone systems, automotive products that reduce pollution and increase gas mileage, water filters, herbal tonics, investment opportunities, memberships, travel clubs, etc., your product or service is the single most important aspect of your business.

Products are *the* driving force for a Network Marketing Distributor's business. And the very best products will enhance or even change people's lives for the better.

Now, here's a revelation from the upper realms of marketing wisdom:

Almost every product has life enhancing benefits.

"Well," you say, "If that's the case, why isn't almost *every* product a great success?"

Good question. Here's why: Because the people offering the product or service do not say the *right things* to the *right people.*

They don't show and tell people what the real *benefits* of their products or services are, or specifically, what the product or service will do for the customer.

How do you know what the right things to say are, and who are the right people to say them to?

Another good question, and what's more, it's the second part of your three-part New Distributor Training program.

PRODUCT KNOWLEDGE

Now, every effective New Distributor Training program gets your new distributors to participate as much as possible right from the start.

What I like to do is pass out a *Product Benefits Worksheet.* (An example of this worksheet is in Chapter Ten). Everybody in that New Distributor Training program has this worksheet. Here is how we use it.

BENEFITS

What we do now is creative brainstorming. Right there in that training program, we collectively discover the benefits people will enjoy when using these products.

Now this is very important. We do *not* talk about all the facts or the features, and the technical data. We talk about *the benefits* people will enjoy. The benefits are *the results* they'll get when they use the product or service.

Too often, people get caught up in some feature of the product or some technical detail with which they themselves are fascinated. These facts are only important to support the benefits people will get from using the products. People want to know what your product or service *will do for them*.

That it contains this or that ingredient may be very interesting, and it may make a real contribution to the product's value, but your prospects want to know in what way this product will make a difference in their lives.

Do you remember that tremendously successful AT&T ad campaign, "Reach out and touch someone," or McDonalds' "You deserve a break today"? Not a feature was ever mentioned. Those commercials were *pure benefits*. That's what I ask you to focus on.

So in this brainstorming session, everybody just calls out a benefit, and the leader writes the benefits down on a flip chart (people can copy them down on their lists later). When you do this, the energy in the room is fantastic!

Now, in brainstorming it's important not to say "No"

to anything. Nothing stops the free flow of ideas like, "No, you're wrong."

Later there will be time to correct any misconceptions. For now, you get all your new distributors to brainstorm as to what benefits people will enjoy. It's important that it come from them—and that's a big part of what's happening here. After this session, they really "own" these benefits.

The truth is, you will probably learn something new every time you do this exercise. And when *you* can take your new distributors with all of their basic, raw enthusiasm, and just help them become more successful in communicating the product's benefits, you will increase their sales effectiveness and productivity *at least* tenfold.

COMMON QUESTIONS

Next, you teach every new distributor how to answer the most commonly asked questions about your product or service.

You can have a typed or printed list of these questions with good, solid responses as to how to answer them successfully.

Make sure your new distributors, who have all this great, but very vulnerable enthusiasm, are fully prepared to answer these questions. Don't make them go through the school of hard knocks by finding out what works and what doesn't work out in the field. Your job is to take care of them. And if you're bringing them into this opportunity, you should know what some of the most commonly asked questions about your products are.

Now, you can also have a brainstorming session to generate these commonly asked questions or to add to the list you've already made up. Again, as with the session you did for the product benefits, have them call out the questions, and you and the more seasoned distributors can add to them if necessary.

After the questions come the answers. Again, you can have some already printed up, but allow your new distributors to contribute additional answers in a brainstorming session.

Also, here's a great place for role-playing. You can make up teams or have people get into pairs with each other to ask and answer these common questions. The energy is terrific. People really get a handle on what they need to know and how they can express their enthusiasm in the most productive manner.

If you prepare your new people to answer those frequently asked questions, you're preparing them for the real world. You're going to minimize their feelings of rejection and discouragement within those first few weeks of being in the business. And when you do that, *your Network's drop-out rate will drop way down—and your sales percentage will soar.*

One other thing about product knowledge:

DON'T FORGET YOUR COMPANY

This is probably more true for Network Marketing than for conventional businesses: *a great product comes from a great company.*

It's easy for new people to become enthusiastic about your company and its people.

If you want a model of someone who has unshakable faith in your product or service—look at the principals of your company. Their commitment to the products, and to you, is what got them where they are today. Their leadership is what keeps you and your company going.

Every great Network Marketing company has some pretty great people up at the top. The ones I've met understand that as much as your distributor business is product driven, *their* business is *distributor driven*. That means that they focus their attention, creativity and support on making your job as easy and successful for you as possible. The men and women who lead your company are as important a part of the real value of your product or service as if they were one of the ingredients. In fact, they are.

Because many Network Marketing products need to be experienced to be enjoyed, a big part of the product information you convey to people will be about the company itself. So, make sure you invest some time on this too. It can be a very big part of your new distributors' enthusiasm, and it's especially useful when you get to the "Presentation" part of your New Distributor Training.

WHO'S MOST LIKELY...

Another exercise you can use is a really powerful way to get your people cooking. This is a worksheet of "Product Benefits and Who's Most Likely To Use My Product or Service." (An example of this worksheet is in the back of

Chapter Ten). This is a perfect place for brainstorming as well.

In brainstorming product benefits, you taught your new distributors the right thing to say; now you're teaching them about who are the right people to say it to.

Link up "who's most likely" with the benefits you listed earlier. Your group will generate a tremendous number of possibilities from this exercise. Because they're focused on the benefits, they'll discover more people who can enjoy the products. More than they would have ever thought of before.

That's it. That's all we do about the products. I told you this system was simple.

Now, the "Who's Most Likely…" exercise is great for ending the product section, because it flows so well into the next section.

BUSINESS KNOWLEDGE

That's what we'll talk about in the very next chapter. The Business Knowledge section begins with "Prospecting."

Chapter Five:
Prospecting

So, now you understand the first steps of your training program, your people have a good foundation in the product and are ready to get into business knowledge. Now the business section is not about the compensation plan. It's about actually "doing" the business. In this chapter, we'll explore the nuts and bolts of prospecting. Prospecting is the life blood of your business. And as you'll learn, the difference between prospecting and selling is one thing that makes Network Marketing the most unique and powerful "sales and distribution" system in the world.

I want to tell you a secret. Now, get ready, this is going to blow your mind.

Let's say I own a gold mine. That's right, a gold mine. And it is, in fact, one of the richest gold mines in the world.

Now I'm going to make you a very special offer. I'm going to tell you where my gold mine is, so you can go in and take out all the gold you want.

Let me repeat that. I'm letting you have all the gold you want. There's just one catch. You're only allowed to go in and come out of my mine *once*.

So, what are you going to do first? Are you going to rush right in and see how much you can take out with your bare hands and raw enthusiasm? That's one way. But if you're smart, you'll go home and get all the tools you'll need to prospect a fortune.

Well, I actually do have that gold mine. So do you. It's Network Marketing. And if you're going to be a master prospector, you'll need to work with the tools a master prospector uses. That's what this chapter is about.

First of all...

WHAT IS A PROSPECTOR?

Do you have the same image appear in your mind as I do when you hear the word "prospector?" Some grizzly, bearded old guy in dirty rumpled overalls, pulling a mule over-burdened with picks, shovels and supplies—right?

Well, that's what a prospector used to look like.

Today, it's a lot different. And the job of prospecting is even more different than that old picture as well.

There are a few key words in the definition of "prospector" upon which I ask you to focus. A prospector is one who *explores* an *area* for *natural valuables* such as gold, oil or diamonds.

So, what's prospecting? Exploring, for one. Not making, creating, convincing, persuading or selling— *exploring.*

And you explore an *area*. What are the boundaries of your "area?" With the exception of the marketing rights of your Network Marketing company, the only boundaries are in your mind.

What is a prospector looking for? "Natural Valuables." Not something that has to be made or created, something *natural*, something which already exists. And something of great value, too. Something that's as precious as gold or oil or diamonds.

Let me tell you one of the most famous stories in all of Network Marketing. It's told by the master story teller, the late Earl Nightingale—founder of Nightingale-Conant—which has for years produced some of the finest teaching and motivational cassette tapes in the world. The story is called...

ACRES OF DIAMONDS

No one knows for sure who told this story first, but it's supposed to be true—and of course, it is—because it has happened thousands of times to thousands of people in thousands of different situations.

The man who made the story famous (in this country, at least) was Dr. Russell Herman Conwell, who lived from 1843 to 1925. By telling the story from one end of the world to another, Conwell raised $6 million, with which he founded Temple University in Philadelphia. He thus fulfilled his dream of building a really fine school for poor but deserving young men.

Conwell told "Acres of Diamonds" more than 6,000 times and attracted great audiences wherever he appeared. I'm sure you're as familiar with the story as I am. But it isn't the story itself that's so important (and you're probably wondering if I'm ever going to get around to telling it!)—the important thing is to apply the principle of the story to our own lives.

"Acres of Diamonds" is about a farmer who lived in Africa at the time when diamonds were discovered. When a visitor told him of the millions being made by men who were discovering diamond mines, he promptly sold his farm and left to search for diamonds himself.

Well, he wandered all over the continent, but found no diamonds. Finally—penniless, in poor health and despondent—he threw himself into a river and drowned.

Long before he met his miserable end, the man who had bought the farm from him found a large, unusual looking stone in the creek bed which ran through the farm. He put it on his mantle as a curio.

Enter the same visitor who had told the original farmer about the diamond discoveries. He examined the stone, and told the farm's new owner that he had discovered one of the largest diamonds ever found, and that it was worth a king's ransom. To his surprise, this farmer replied, "Oh, my entire farm is covered with stones just like that one."

To make a long story short, the farm—which the first farmer had sold so he could go off searching for diamonds—turned out to be one of the richest diamond mines in the world.

The point Dr. Conwell made was that the first farmer had already owned acres of diamonds—but had made the mistake of not examining what he had before running off to something he hoped would be better.

As Dr. Conwell would point out, each of us is like that first farmer. No matter where we live or what we do, we are surrounded by acres of diamonds—if we'll simply look for them. Like the curious-looking stones that covered the farm, they might not appear to be diamonds at first glance. But a little study—a deeper examination and some polishing—will reveal our opportunities and our abilities for what they really are.

So, now you understand clearly what this chapter is all about. We're going to go exploring a vast, unlimited area in your own backyard, full of already existing precious natural valuables.

Sound like fun? Great, let's go!

THE PROSPECT LIST

The first "business" thing I like to teach in a new distributor training program—and again I pull out a worksheet—is the *Prospect List*. (An example of this worksheet is in Chapter Ten). I physically get people to go through the exercise of exploring all their natural and valuable prospects right there in the training program.

I have not yet met a successful individual in this business who didn't work off of a tangible prospect list. So, right in your training program, you have them start making out that list. And after they make it out, you'll teach them how to prioritize it.

ONE HUNDRED NAMES OR MORE

Have each new distributor list *everyone* he or she can think of on the prospect list. I always suggest a *minimum* of 100 names. And that really isn't hard to do, because according to statistics, most men and women 21 or older actually know more than *700 people!*

If any people experience difficulty in getting up to a hundred names, try this:

Have them get out their personal phone book (and of course, make sure you tell them to bring this to the training) and write all the names in that book on their list. Have them take out any business cards they've collected and write those names and numbers down, too.

Then have them ask themselves these questions:

"Whom do I know because of my work?… because of my children?… because of my interests and hobbies?… because of my church?…" etc.

Take them back to the "Who's Most Likely To Use My Product" list to generate more names as well.

If they need more help in filling out their list, call a brainstorming session. They can do this on their own too.

Just have them get two or five family members and friends around and ask them to help generate names for their prospect list. Your new distributors will be amazed and delighted at how these other people will help jog their memory—and even come up with 20, 30 or more names and places to look for prospects that hadn't occured to them before.

Remember, we're exploring here. So don't let them say "No" to any names for their list. We'll get to priorities in just a minute. For now, everybody and anybody is perfect.

WHY 100 NAMES?
Let me explain it this way.

The most common mistake made by new distributors is that when they first make that decision to go out there and start talking to people about the product and opportunity, three, four or five people they know immediately come to mind. They don't write these people down, they just think of three or four or five people. Then they immediately pick up the phone and call one of them.

Chances are that person may not be interested for a variety of reasons, most of which have nothing to do with your new distributor. And if their first phone call is to someone who's not interested, that's one out of three or one out of five people who say "No." They've just lost 20 or 30 percent of their prospects! That's a real bad start. But when you have a list of 100 people, and you call up that first person and for whatever reason he or she isn't interested, you can easily say, "That's okay, I'll just check you off my list for now." One percent. No big deal.

You see why 100 names is so important?

Remember two things: First, we're prospecting. We're exploring all the possibilities to discover precisely where to look for gold.

The second point is, SW, SW, SW—NEXT. Some Will, Some Won't, So What—NEXT! A list of five people doesn't give you very many "Nexts."

PROSPECTING: STEP TWO—PRIORITIES

Now, the reason you prioritize your list is that you want to select those people who are going to be the most receptive, the most open to what you have to offer.

So the first group you can have people select—the "A's"—are the *people-people*. These are the high-energy types, the bubbly people who are always fun to be around. They're able to attract people to them by virtue of their happy, friendly personalities. And when they get excited about something—they tell the world!

My sister is one of them. I'm so proud of her. She's the first millionaire in our family. She's in real estate development and I'm convinced that she's succeeded in great part by virtue of her bubbly, vibrant personality.

People just love to be around her. She's so bright, so happy—and she absolutely loves people. She has a magnetic personality that just attracts people to her. And she attracts other things as well. Her last commission check was well over a $1 million! Imagine that. And all because she's bubbly. Well, she's obviously very smart and knows her business, too, but *who* and *how* she is, is a big part of her success.

The next group—the "B's"—are the *positive people*. The easiest way to identify them is to go over your list and put a check by the names of the people who are negative. Don't cross them off the list. (By the way, people who always say, "Now, let's be realistic," are probably negative types.) Just leave them alone for now.

The "C's" are the *successful people*, people who are doing really well in their lives and their work. Don't prejudge these people. Make them a high priority.

It's a common mistake to avoid successful people because we assume they're too busy, don't "need" the money, etc. However, successful people are the most likely to recognize a good opportunity when they see one. Remember, successful people have a successful circle of influence—and if they like what they see, they'll be off and running in the business before you know it. And you want your people to set up their list for success. So train them to go for the winners first.

By the way, if you notice a bubbly, positive, very *successful* person—like my sister—put him or her on the very top of your list!

LONG DISTANCE LOVE AFFAIRS

Don't prejudge anyone on the list because they live far away from you either. As long as they are within the marketing rights of your company and your distributorship, give them the priority they deserve. With the proper follow-up system (which we'll talk about in Chapter Eight: Follow Through), it doesn't matter if your prospect is next door to you or 3000 miles away. Except for the rates, the telephone has no real understanding of distance.

One of the great things about Network Marketing is that you can build a truly successful, national business *over the phone.*

Nothing is more effective for transferring enthusiasm than the spoken voice. So don't limit your thinking—or speaking—to your own back yard. Besides, with the new telecommunication technologies of "demand conference calling," fax machines and the like, more and more Network Marketers will be reaching out and touching more and more people. Pretty soon, we'll reach out and touch *everyone!*

Using the telephone is the third step in your basic prospecting system.

PROSPECTING: STEP THREE— PICK UP THE PHONE

Here's where you invite your priority prospects to learn about your product and opportunity.

The User Friendly Phone. Now, you may have one of those unusual telephones that sometimes weighs 250 pounds. For some people, the phone can be a cold and impersonal thing. You need to make it more friendly.

One thing I like to suggest is to get a mirror in front of you and write a big "SMILE" in lipstick across the top of it. Then make your calls looking at yourself in that mirror with that big SMILE.

One student of mine got over her "phone-fears" by cutting out pictures from magazines of people laughing, smiling and hugging each other and pasting them all over her mirror and phone. Have fun—write yourself little inspirational messages and affirmations—like, "Wow, thanks so much for calling," or "What a great opportunity, I'm thrilled you called!"—and stick them all over the place where you make your calls.

THE PHONE IS FOR APPOINTMENTS

Now, the phone should be used primarily for scheduling appointments—*not for making presentations.* Too often, we try to sell people over the phone, and the phone isn't the best way to make a "sales" presentation, unless you're a professional telemarketer.

There are some exceptions to this rule. Exception number one would be when the person to whom you're talking to lives 2500 miles away!

Another exception is if you happen to have a product that's especially affordable for most people—a product that people can easily try. Here you can have your prospects agree to let you send them out a sample of the product to use and see for themselves how great it is. Here's how you do that.

Tell your prospects about the product—not all the features, just how great you think it is, and how the other people you've shared it with think so, too. Share your enthusiasm and personal experience with them. Tell them you value their opinion, and that you want to know what they think. Ask if you can send them some information and a sample, and if they like it as much as you do, they can send you back a check. If they don't, for any reason, they can simply send back the product. Of course, you may want to do this only with high priority prospects.

USE THE MONEY-BACK GUARANTEE

Many Network Marketing companies offer a satisfaction money-back guarantee. It's common policy, and required by law in many states when you "sell" something over the phone or through the mail.

Now, it's a part of human nature that most of us don't feel good about asking for our money back. And that, combined with the fact that most Network Marketing products *really are special and really do work,* makes this approach a fairly secure thing to do. Also, if you're genuinely excited about a product and it's getting results for you, the odds are most everybody else will enjoy trying it, too.

Remember the scientifically proven "placebo effect"? One third of the people will get positive results, one third will not get any results, and one third won't really know if they did or not. Network Marketing companies usually offer such great products that they can actually double that percentage of positive results—sometimes 60 percent or higher. And if you've "qualified" your prospects with the priorities I mentioned before, you can do just as well—or perhaps even better.

So, if you have a product that retails for $20 to $70, and it has a money-back guarantee, most people will be willing to take the chance of trying it based on your personal recommendation. Just tell them you want them to try it for a few days, and that you'll enclose an invoice, and if they get true value and benefit from it and they really like it, they can pay you for it.

FIVE FACTORS FOR EFFECTIVELY USING YOUR TELEPHONE

There are five ingredients I recommend you incorporate into all your telephone invitations. Using them will increase your effectiveness tremendously. Here they are:

1. "Is this a good time?"
2. Transfer enthusiasm.
3. Compliment your prospect.
4. Offer a disclaimer.
5. Close your objective.

Let's talk about each one of them.

1. "IS THIS A GOOD TIME?"

Have you ever had someone call you when you didn't want to talk? What kind of reception did you give them? How well did you listen and how open were you to what they were saying? We've all had it happen.

So, point one, find out if this is a good time to talk. It's an appreciated courtesy, and more—it makes sure you get the listening you deserve.

2. TRANSFER ENTHUSIASM

Most people think that communication is a transfer of information from one person to the next. And for limited purposes—it is. But truly effective communication requires transfering *enthusiasm*, not just information.

What you say certainly is important. But I believe that

how you feel about what you say is the most important thing of all.

You don't have to become an expert about all the facts and features of your product, your company, or your marketing plan to be a powerful communicator. In fact, being that kind of expert may actually *block* real and effective communication.

Please remember, this is the duplication business. It's far easier to learn to share enthusiasm than to attempt to transfer years of acquired knowledge.

The more excited and enthusiastic you are, the more likely and quickly you'll be successful. As I said before, the key to the word enthusiasm is the last four letters— I A S M—I Am Sold Myself. You have to be your own best customer! If you find more and more people aren't interested in your product or opportunity—look first to your own enthusiasm. I'll bet it's begun to wane.

You know, there's an old sales adage that says, when you first start out, you're 90 percent enthusiasm and 10 percent knowledge. After a while it changes to 90 percent knowledge and 10 percent enthusiasm. Just before that time, either you do something to up that enthusiasm percentage—or you should start looking for another product or service to work with.

3. COMPLIMENT YOUR PROSPECT

The reason this is important is that when you extend a compliment to your prospects over the phone, you accomplish two things.

First, you have now set clearly in their minds why it

was so important for you to contact *them*. And second: you really have their attention!

Do you listen any differently to someone who calls you and starts talking about what they want to say, versus someone who calls you and says he or she really values your opinion, because you're such a professional, or because you have such a great sense of quality or good taste? It works.

4. OFFER A DISCLAIMER

How many times has someone tried to sell you something by selling you, selling you, selling you, selling you... The more they push, the more you shut down. It's natural. We all do it for protection, if nothing else.

Allow your prospect to feel there is no obligation in meeting with you. Give your prospect the space to let his or her natural curiosity come to the fore. And let them know this isn't for everybody. That'll get their interest up.

5. CLOSE YOUR OBJECTIVE

The last point is to get what you want from the call.

If your objective is to set an appointment, offer them a choice of times and days you know would be good for your prospect to meet with you. Don't ask them..."when can we get together?" If your objective is to send them a promo package or a sample, then assume that's what they want. Tell them what you're going to do and ask them where they want you to send it.

Always come from the assumption that they want

what you have to offer. When you do that, more often than not—they will.

Now, let's give an example of how these five ingredients all blend together.

"Hi Betty, this is John Kalench. Is this a convenient time for us to talk for a couple of minutes? It is? Great!

"Betty, the reason I'm calling is, I'm so excited about something I just got involved with. I thought of you because of the way people feel about you and respect you, I know you can do extremely well with this.

"Now I can't make any guarantees Betty. I'm not completely sure this is something that's right for you. What I would like to do is just sit down together for a few minutes and share some ideas. I think you'll see a fantastic opportunity here. I believe you'll see ways we can have a lot of fun with this and how we can make a lot of money together.

"So, I'm buying lunch this week Betty. Which day is best for you, Tuesday or Thursday?"

Now, that has all of the five ingredients you want in a call.

I recommend that you prepare a script for the calls you're going to make. Not to sound like a computer—just to write down an outline of those key points: why your calling her (why Betty's important to you), why it may not be right for her, what you want to do, and finally, give her a choice of when to get together.

With a simple outline script in front of you, you don't

have to exert effort to remember what you're going to say. You can focus on transferring your enthusiasm.

SOME COMMON QUESTIONS

Now, you're frequently going to be asked some questions.

If someone asks you, "What is it?" my strong recommendation is: *tell them. Don't try to avoid that question!*

Tell them the name of the company, the name of the product, and be prepared to give a one or two-sentence description of what the company does or what the product is, and then go right back into closing your objective. Don't rush this, either. Avoiding the answer or sounding like you wish they'd never asked isn't a good message to communicate.

If you're genuinely enthusiastic, you'll gladly answer and move along to what you really want to talk about. If you're not, your prospect will pick it up for sure. People have a built-in insincerity alarm. It goes off loud and clear when it hears avoidance.

The most valuable quality you have in this industry is your integrity and your word. So when you're asked a question, answer it straight, short and true—and then move forward once again to your objective.

"I'M BUSY"

You might get a response such as, "Well, I don't know, John, I'm very busy... I don't think I'd be interested in this." Then you can say:

"Betty, I can definitely appreciate that. I know you're

busy. That's one reason why I called you. You're the kind of woman who gets things done. Look, Betty, if you don't see within a matter of 20 or 25 minutes, something that really excites you, I promise I won't bring it up to you again. So I'm still buying lunch, which day is best for you, Tuesday or Thursday?"

And if she doesn't see any value after your presentation—don't pressure her.

Keep your word with people.

"I'M NOT INTERESTED"

Okay, here's what you do with this one.

Find out, specifically, *what it is* that doesn't interest them. Ask a question like;

"Betty, I can appreciate that. Just for my benefit, would you tell me what part of this it is that you're not interested in? Is it the product and the benefits it offers? Is it the business opportunity?"

Now, if they say it's the business opportunity, you can tell them you understand and encourage them to give the product a try, based on the benefits you're excited about along with your money-back guarantee.

However, sometimes a statement like this is a smoke screen for something else.

Maybe it's a difficult time for them in their lives. Perhaps they're one of the people who's had a problem with a "bad" or inappropriate opportunity in our industry. Whatever it is, do your best to pin down what they're not interested in and why.

If they are *flat out* not interested at all—fine. Give them room to be that way. *Do not pressure them!* And always leave an opening to get back in touch.

KEEPING IN TOUCH

"Well, Betty, I understand that you're not interested now. But I really value your opinion, so I'd like to keep in touch with you. Would you be open to me calling you again and letting you know how I'm doing maybe a month or so down the road?"

Get a commitment from this person that they would have no objection with your keeping in touch.

Most of the time, a "not interested" response simply means that the timing is not right for them. Nothing succeeds like success—and as you become more successful, they may become more open. The time may be right for them sooner than either of you imagined.

And remember, we're in the sorting business. So...

SW, SW, SW—NEXT!

Keeping in communication with people is a real key to your success.

Many times I've been approached by a distributor when the timing just wasn't right for me. But he or she kept in touch. And often, after a couple months, I was more open to what they had to offer. And it's true, people love to share each other's success. Just hearing about somebody who's doing really well picks me up and makes me smile. Make sure to keep the lines of communication open and share your success with people. It's powerful!

Some experts say that people don't respond until the fourth or fifth contact. I don't know if that's completely accurate, but I do know that persistence and what I call "relentless patience" pays off. Again, this is a case of "Do It."

Also, always—no matter what the outcome of the call—thank them.

Thank them for their opinion, thank them for their support, thank them for their valuable time. Pay them a compliment if you can. This is a sure-fire way to have them be happy to hear from you the next time you call.

ANOTHER APPROACH—ASK FOR ADVICE

A really successful way to introduce someone to an opportunity, and one that beautifully combines all of the key ingredients, is to ask for their advice. This works particularly well with family members, friends and even acquaintances whose backgrounds or experience makes them somebody whose opinion you value.

Simply tell them that you're considering starting or have just started your own business, and you want to show them your product or opportunity and get their opinion. People love to give advice, especially if you elevate them to the position of being an expert on the subject. Chances are, they'll see the value you see in your product and/or opportunity. Now your "expert" just became your customer or distributor!

I recommend that you prepare one basic phone script for family and close friends, and another for acquaintances and people you don't know that well. You just choose different words for the different categories of prospects.

LEARN TO LOVE YOUR TELEPHONE

A very wise person once said: *The speed by which we manifest the things we want in life is directly proportionate to the speed with which we become comfortable with those things.*

The sooner you make a friend of that 250-pound, "user friendly" phone of yours, the sooner you'll be able to use its awesome power to build your business with the greatest success. Make a commitment to call a specific number of prospects per day, per week, per month—and do it! You'll be amazed how light that phone becomes in just a couple of days or weeks. One thing I strongly suggest is to get a phone you really like and enjoy using. They have all kinds of terrific new phones available now.

THE NEVER ENDING PROSPECT LIST

When I first got started in this business, I made a list of 100 names and went to work immediately. I scheduled appointments and made a number of presentations with my "A" priority prospects. And an amazing thing happened.

Many of my "A" prospects got involved using the products, but didn't enroll in the business opportunity right away. However, what they did was give me four or five referrals of family and friends they thought would enjoy using the products. Before I realized what was happening, my list was 150 people long—*and it was filling up with new "A" people given to me by my prospects!*

It took me ages to get all the way down to my "B's" and "C's." And what's more, once I had four or five of my prospects' referrals started on the products and interested in the opportunity, I went back to my original prospects and showed them that they already had a going business if they wanted it. And most of them did.

And you know what? All those referrals were strangers I never knew before!

YOUR "WARM MARKET"

I haven't been completely happy with the term we use in Network Marketing to describe the family and friends who make up the majority of our prospect lists in the beginning. If there's such a thing as a "warm market," that means there must be a "cold market" as well. I don't buy that. The only cold market is Iceland.

The fact is, sooner or later—and in truth for most of us in this business it's sooner—you'll be talking to and prospecting "strangers" to build your business. Think about this.

Two to three years from today, you'll have a large and prosperous Network Marketing business. You'll have, say, 50 to 100 leaders and an organization of thousands. Do you have any idea how many of these people you know right now? The fact is, you haven't met most of them yet!

THE SORTING BUSINESS

Again, this business isn't a matter of convincing people. It's a matter of sorting through them to find the ones who are ready for your product and opportunity.

I remember when I was a kid watching the half-time interviews during a pro football game. They were talking with an all-pro defensive lineman with the Baltimore

Colts, named Earl "Big Daddy" Lipscomb. He was very big and very good. The sportscaster asked him, "Earl, how do you explain your uncanny ability to tackle the ball carrier? Big Daddy gave this huge grin and said, "It's easy. I just tackle them all until I find the one with the ball." He was in the sorting business, too.

Remember, it's prospecting—you're exploring for already existing valuables. The phone is one of the very best ways to sort through your prospects quickly and get your business on the fast track to success.

Now, what about prospecting other than with the telephone?

~~DON'T~~ TALK TO STRANGERS

Why does the idea of talking to strangers frighten so many people? Do you suppose that cautious little message we received as kids, "Don't talk to strangers," became so ingrained in our consciousness that even as adults we still won't do it?

Well, whatever the reason, sooner or later successful Network Marketers do talk to strangers—and they have a ball doing it too.

HOW TO MAKE THE WORLD YOUR OYSTER

There's a world full of pearls out there. Right now, they're all strangers. How do you reach them? How do you get past any existing barriers to creating an ever-increasing flow of new and prosperous relationships? How do you make friends out of strangers?

The answer to this question is one of the very best parts of this entire book. The answer is...*have fun!*

That's what it takes. Do you want to have fun? Great! Here are a bunch of fun things to do.

BE A WALKING BILLBOARD FOR YOUR PRODUCTS AND OPPORTUNITY

If it's possible, carry your products with you. When around strangers, pull them out—display them where you sit—mix them up—offer people a taste or feel—dangle them in front of people—drop them in their laps if you have to (just kidding).

My point is this: get people's attention whenever and wherever possible. Get people to express an interest and ask you questions. You are in the advertising business as well—so advertise!

Buttons are wonderful. That's right—buttons. If your company has them, wear them. Especially if they solicit a response from people.

To tell you the truth, this is one of those ideas I didn't believe at first. But experience changed my opinion. Buttons work so well, it's amazing!

One company used to have a button that said, "Lose weight now, ask me how." I've talked to distributors who say the the only thing they ever did to prospect for new customers and distributors was to walk around the mall with that button on and speak to people who came up to them and asked, "How?"

A very successful woman I know who was with a water filter company wore a button that said, "Bottled water for just 3¢ a gallon." She said people would come up to her in the supermarket with five, one-dollar-per gallon jugs of bottled water in their carts and ask if her button was *really* telling the truth. She *rarely* goes anywhere without her button. Her business earns her family more than $260,000 a year!

If your company doesn't have buttons, you can make them yourself. Simple button machines are inexpensive, and many button companies are so reasonably priced that you can get a couple of your distributors together and have whatever you want made up for you.

Bumper stickers are another way. Even signs in the window of your car can work magic.

One distributor, who drives a Mercedes provided by his company, has a sign in each of the side windows that says, "I got this car *FREE*—Ask me how to get yours." And his phone number is on the sign. He gets an average of eight calls a week.

Buttons, bumper stickers, decals, note pads, hats, tee-shirts, post cards... these are just some of the ways you can get your message out to people in a fun and compelling way that has *them call you*. Be creative and have fun. People love it when you do!

And speaking of creative fun, listen to this.

DORIS' DOORKNOBS

A very dear friend of mine, and of the entire Network Marketing industry, is Doris Wood. Doris has been the President of our industry trade association—the Multi-level Marketing International Association (MLMIA) for the past seven years. She's been a million dollar distributor and is currently a highly sought after consultant. Doris absolutely refuses to do anything that isn't fun.

Here's a fun trick she's used for years.

She goes into a hardware store and asks to look at all the doorknobs. Then she picks one out that suits her style—for Doris, that means elegant crystal. It may be brass, wood or whatever you choose. Then she takes it with her everywhere she goes.

If she's in a store, she puts it right up on the counter. In a restaurant or coffee shop, it sits right out on the table. She takes it on planes, in her car, everywhere. Now, people simply cannot resist asking Doris what the doorknob is for. That's her cue. Doris looks right at them, smiles, flashes her big, twinkling eyes and says,

"I'm *so* happy you asked me that. This doorknob is to remind me to tell you that the door to opportunity is wide open for you with..." then she adds the name of her company or product. And she's off and running.

Isn't that great!

Doris is a master of one thing that can make you successful in Network Marketing. She understands *human nature*. She knows most people aren't having fun in their jobs. And she also knows that people cannot resist a person who *is* having fun. She knows that the toughest part of talking to strangers is to work up the courage to speak to them. So, she sets it up so they speak to *her* first! It's brilliant.

A NEW WAY TO PAY YOUR BILLS

Close your eyes for a moment and imagine what the men and women do, all day long, who receive your bill payments. Not very exciting, is it?

What if they got a flyer or a personal note from you, along with your check, that invited them to try your product or service, or learn about a fantastic business opportunity? You're already sending them money and you've paid for the postage anyway. Try it.

In fact, don't let one piece of correspondence leave your house without including a message about your product or business. It's a simple, cost effective way to get your product and opportunity in front of hundreds of new people.

FIRST IMPRESSIONS

You know the value and importance of first impressions. As the saying goes, you only get one chance to make a first impression.

Did you know that the average person makes as many as 40 distinct decisions about you within the first few minutes of meeting you? I think that's incredible! How you look, smile, make or do not make eye contact, your grooming, what you say and how you say it, how well you listen, your body language... all that and more is, in a very real sense, on trial in those first two or three minutes.

There is much material available on how to make a good first impression. Far too much and too many ideas to go into in this book. Let me list a couple of resources here that will be a big help to you.

My number one favorite is one of the first and still one of the best: Dale Carnegie's *How To Win Friends And Influence People*. There's so much proven practical wisdom in this one book. It's the best.

Jack Trout and Al Ries have written a classic marketing text called *Positioning: The Battle For Your Mind*. This book can tell you a great deal about how to "position" yourself and make great impressions. It's also very valuable for understanding all about positioning your product and business opportunity—because the very same rules apply.

Dressing To Win by Robert Panté is a good one for having an understanding of how to use clothing to present yourself in the best possible fashion. And if you're up for a deeper, text-book approach using the science of Neuro Linguistic Programming (NLP), Genie Laborde's *Influencing With Integrity* is excellent. We'll talk about some of her principles a little later on, when we get to building rapport with people.

Remember: Education and Knowledge. That's what make Al and Alice Achiever such happy and successful campers—and Network Marketers.

SO, WHAT DO YOU DO?

Imagine yourself at a social event or party and you're being introduced to people you've never met before. People will inevitably ask, "What do you do for a living?" or, "What kind of work do you do?" What do you say? This is your golden opportunity to advertise and make a positive and compelling first impression.

I have an exercise in one of the workshops we do where I have people create a couple of different answers to this question.

One man I worked with was a very successful salesman from the insurance business, and he'd been in Network Marketing with a nutrition company for a number of months. He was doing okay, but not as well as he thought he could. So, he volunteered to come up in front of the room and I asked him what he did for a living. He gave me two different answers:

"I'm an MLM distributor"—and, "I'm with XYZ company. We sell a line of quack, quack, quack..." Well, that was a pretty ho-hum beginning. So, we worked on doing it differently. Here's what he came up with:

"I'm in the Health and Wealth business. Which one would you like to hear about first?"

Isn't that great! I saw him two months later, and his business had absolutely taken off!

It won't take you very long at all to come up with a couple of dynamite answers to the question of what you do for a living. You can tailor a response that really speaks to your personality. One immediate result you'll experience is an increase in your confidence. I promise you, working on this will be some of the most productive minutes you ever invest in your business.

THE MOST IMPORTANT FIRST IMPRESSION

Here's something I ask you to tattoo on the inside of your head, right up there in the forefront of your mind:

People don't care how much you know, until they know how much you care.

In other words...learn to get out of yourself, and into other people first.

Ask questions...and listen intently to the answers.

This is perhaps the biggest, most powerful key to success in this business—and in life as well.

IT'S ALL A GAME

Prospecting is a game. For that matter, so is life!

I don't say that to make light of either one. I say that to have you understand that when you approach prospecting—or life—with the spirit of creativity, play and fun, it takes on a whole new and exciting dimension.

Prospecting is a numbers game. Once you learn the principles and some tips and techniques—like the ones in this chapter—it becomes a matter of *the more people you talk to, the more success you'll have.* It's as simple as that.

The way to guarantee failure in this business is not to talk to enough people. The way to guarantee success in this business is to talk to more and more people. You may have to stretch your comfort zone to accomplish this. Fine. Do it. Why? Because when you make a habit of making friends out of strangers, making money will become a habit with you.

Just make a game of it.

Go down to the hardware store and buy 10 little ball

bearings. Stick them in your pocket or purse. Every time you talk to a stranger for any reason take out one ball and transfer it to another pocket. And don't go to bed that night until your first pocket is empty!

Don't worry about what to say. You don't have to talk about your business or products in the beginning. Just strike up a conversation about anything at all.

Your success is simply measured by the number of new people you try to meet. Pretty soon, you'll get to the point where you are so comfortable talking with strangers, that at least five to ten people a day will want to know more about you and what you do. When you start this game, all you have to do is have a conversation. And every time you do, no matter how small or short, transfer one ball. Each ball transfered is a success, regardless of the outcome. In a matter of weeks you'll be a master at making friends out of strangers. And then you'll have all the prospects you could ever want for your products and business. Even more importantly, you will have made... "the world your oyster."

And remember, SW, SW, SW—NEXT! (Some will—Some won't—So what—NEXT). A Master Prospector is a Master Game Player.

Now, how about becoming a Master of Presentations, too? Would you like to do that? Great—turn the page.

Chapter Six:
Your Presentation

Now it's time for the face-to-face aspect of your person-to-person business—The Presentation. Here's where you get "belly-button to belly-button" with your prospect. This is one of the most fundamental parts of every distributor's business and training. Would you like to know a way to make all your presentations an effortless, effective joy? Read on.

The presentation is the foundation of your business. I'm not talking about an opportunity meeting. That's different, and we'll talk about that soon. This is the one-on-one presentation. Or perhaps two-on-one. The very small informal meetings.

You've already created a prospect list and prioritized it, and you've learned the required telephone skills so that you can set appointments with "the right people." Now, it's time to learn *how to* say "the right things" to those prospects in your face-to-face meeting.

YOUR PRESENTATION IS A GIFT

When it comes to making presentations, a difficult thing for many of us to do is ask people to commit 30, 40 minutes, or an hour to show them what we have to offer. We feel like we're imposing on them. They're busy and time is very valuable.

I look at it this way. The dictionary defines "presentation" as a performance, or *to offer to another a gift.*

So, every time you sit down with someone and share with them your products, company and opportunity, you're offering that person a gift.

Your time is very valuable too. For you to think enough of yourself and the other person, that you're willing to schedule the time to share with them something you believe to be of great value and benefit to them—that makes you special!

One reason this is important to remember, especially in the beginning, is that you and your new distributors may not always walk away with your prospect's agreement to try your product or to sponsor into your business. But if you're clear that your presentation *is a gift*, you can always feel good about offering it—whether they accept it or not!

What kind of person runs around giving other people gifts all the time? That's right, a good person—and that's the kind of person you are!

REWARD YOURSELF FOR SUCCESS

Here's a little acknowledgement game I teach people that really works!

Set up a separate savings account with your name on it, followed by "Acknowledgment Fund." Every time you give a successful presentation—which means every time you show up and share your gift with someone, no matter what the outcome—you deposit $10 into that account.

Consider it the "applause" you get for making your presentation. By the way, if you get a "standing ovation"— and you will—put in $20.

Now, with 20 or 30 high priority names on your prospect list, you're bound to have a few hundred dollars in your Acknowledgment Fund in a very short time. What should you do with all that money?

Reward yourself. You deserve it!

FIVE STEPS TO EFFECTIVE PRESENTATIONS

Here's a method for giving the most effective and powerful presentations.

Step #1: Get Your Prospects' Attention
Step #2: Discover Their Interest
Step #3: Create The Desire
Step #4: Offer Them A Choice
Step #5: "You Made The Right Choice"

Now, let's go over each step individually.

STEP NUMBER ONE:
GET YOUR PROSPECTS' ATTENTION

As I said in the last chapter, the first impression is the most important. This holds true for presenting just as it does for prospecting. Keep in mind all the things we spoke about before: how you look, how you speak and listen, body language, and especially the fact that *people don't care how much you know until you let them know how much you care.*

That's a key. Here's why.

BUILDING INSTANT RAPPORT

First, you have to get your prospect's attention. Showing them you care is the best and fastest way to do that.

Just as we did when setting up appointments using the telephone, you can extend them a compliment right away. Let them know why they are important to you and why the opportunity to meet with them is special.

Showing your prospect that you appreciate and like them is a quick way to have them appreciate and like you, too.

You can open up the conversation with a genuine,

"How are you?"—and really listen to the answer. For most people, this question is rarely asked or answered sincerely. Just asking and listening intently to the answer lets the person know you care. The answer they give can provide valuable information about them that will help you tailor your presentation to their specific needs and wants.

Don't settle for a glib or cliche response, either. If they toss the answer off, gently press a little.

"Honestly, Bob, how are you?" And be a "committed listener." It's a great beginning. It not only shows that you care enough to ask, it sets a tone for the entire presentation, because right from the start you establish yourself as a *listener*.

And listening, rather than talking, is the key to effective and successful presentations.

God gave us one mouth—and two ears. Do you think He or She was trying to tell us something?

RELAXATION

A kind of background for the whole business of establishing rapport is *comfort*.

When people are ill at ease, uncomfortable or distracted, they don't listen. You've got to have your prospect be *relaxed*.

Maxwell Maltz, the author of the popular and revolutionary book, *Psycho-Cybernetics,* discovered that people are not open to change unless they are in a relaxed state. And no matter what else you want to accomplish with your presentation, you will have to change that person's mind. Even if they are open to you and to what you have to say, your presentation will be changing what they think and how they feel about your product and opportunity. So, relaxation is a real key.

And your behavior is the key to your prospect's level of relaxation.

BE A MIRROR

I won't go into the details of this entire process here. It deserves a whole book all to itself. But mirroring is a simple way for you to have your prospect relaxed, open and happy to hear and see what you have for them.

One key way is to observe your prospect's posture, breathing, gestures and things like that, and then gently mirror them. That means you simply do what your prospect does.

Cross your legs if they have crossed theirs. Sit full front or sideways depending on how they're sitting. Breathe with them, use your hands or facial expressions in a similar fashion, and lean forward or backward with them.

It's subtle and something we all do unconsciously. Simply watch different couples or small groups of people and notice the ones that are mirroring one another.

Language is another key. People tend to express themselves in one dominant way. If you can pick up on their preferred way of speaking, you can create instant rapport, because you will be "coming from" the same orientation they are.

Listen carefully and see which of the following they use most often:

"I see." That shows a visual dominance.

"I hear you." That's auditory.

"I feel." They lead with their emotions.

"I think." These people are more intellectual.

Once you discover this language orientation, you can direct your questions and comments in the way they'll most likely appreciate and understand. "Can you see what I'm talking about?" or "How does that sound to you?" or "How do you feel about what I just said?" or "Well, what do you think about that?"

If you've never done this before, you're in for an amazing revelation.

There is a superb resource for the art and science of building rapport that takes this all much deeper. It's known as Neuro Linguistic Programming (NLP). NLP goes into substantial and very specific detail on mirroring, using syntax, eye movement, skin color changes, and much more to create rapport.

However, I do have a concern and caution about NLP and some of its practitioners. In the "wrong" hands, NLP can be used to manipulate people. That's something I am dead set against. Relationships built on manipulation are doomed to fail.

The art and science of NLP is pure and positive. Like Network Marketing, its principles are sound, even inspired. It's how people apply the principles in practice that makes them either a *contribution to others* or a dishonest *manipulation of others.*

I recommend one book about NLP above all others. The title says it all: *Influencing with Integrity, Management Skills for Communication and Negotiation,* by Genie Z. Laborde (Syntony Publishing, Palo Alto, $21.95).

This is not a "pop" book. It's a real student's text. It's thorough, sensitive and excellent. If you're committed to mastering rapport and communication, this is your book.

"SAY MORE ABOUT THAT"

This is a terrific way to have people tell you more about themselves and what's really important to them.

When you ask them to..."Say more about that" or "Tell me more about that." most people will take this as a sign of you being a caring, intent listener, who has a sincere interest in what they think and feel.

STEP NUMBER TWO: DISCOVER THEIR INTERESTS

One thing you want to accomplish in the initial stages of your presentation is to discover your prospect's real areas of interest. As you do, asking them to "Say more about that" will really help them open up to you. This is important especially with regard to their business experiences and expectations.

After you've established a solid foundation of mutual rapport, ask your prospects if they have ever been in business for themselves. Ask if they've ever been involved with Network Marketing before. If they haven't, ask what they know about it. Use the "Say more about that" technique to fill out their comments so you clearly understand where they stand on the subject.

Get both their positive and negative thoughts and feelings. You'll need this information to successfully accomplish the next point of your presentation.

YOU CAN'T PLEASE ALL THE PEOPLE...

There are some people in this world who are hard to please. Let me tell you a story about one of them.

This man began to frequent one particular restaurant. He was becoming a regular. He always sat at the same table and ordered the same items from the menu.

One of the waiters took a particular interest in this customer. After his meal one evening, the waiter stopped by to ask him how everything was. The man replied that the food and service were fine, but that he really liked bread, and the restaurant only provided one slice. The waiter took note of that fact.

When the man next appeared the waiter made a point of bringing the man two slices of bread before his meal. And again, after the man had finished eating, the waiter stopped by to inquire how his dinner was. The man said the food and the service were quite good, but that he really liked bread, and the waiter had only provided him with two slices. Again, the waiter made a mental note.

The next time the man returned for dinner, the waiter placed a basket of bread, at least four slices, on his table. He made a point of inquiring how the gentleman enjoyed his meal, and again, as before, the man replied that he really liked bread and wished the restaurant was more forthcoming with it.

The waiter went to the manager and they baked up a plan—literally—to satisfy their customer.

On the day the man was expected to return, the baker made a huge loaf of bread. It was more than three feet long! When their customer arrived, the waiter and manager rushed to the kitchen, placed the giant, uncut loaf of bread on top of two serving trays and brought it to the man's table. It literally extended across the table and well over both sides. The waiter and manager stood there beaming, eagerly awaiting the customer's reaction.

The customer looked up at them with a slightly displeased expression and said,

"I can see we're back to only one slice again."

The moral of the story is that sometimes the only satisfaction some people ever get out of life—is in being dissatisfied.

My point: if you find yourself in the company of a Mr. or Ms. "Only One Slice"—please don't waste your time and theirs. Ask them the right questions that reveal what they're up to and then, SW, SW, SW—NEXT. And move on.

STATE YOUR OBJECTIVE

For your open-minded prospects, state your objective up front. For example:

"Now, Bob, what I plan on doing in the next 25 to 30

minutes is sharing with you information about my company, its philosophy and the great people behind it."

"I'm going to show you my products, so you can (taste them, try them, see them—whichever is most appropriate for the kind of products you have). I'm also going to share with you a little bit about the business opportunity behind it. Not all the details, but just enough to give you the flavor of it."

"At the end of this short presentation, Bob, if you don't see anything that truly interests you—I promise you I won't bring it up again. If you do see the value of the products and the business opportunity, then I want to briefly discuss how you can get started. Is that fair?"

Now, with that kind of a preface, people know exactly what to expect. That helps them to be relaxed and open. They know what you expect of them as well, so they're not surprised at the end when you ask them if they want to try the products or participate in your opportunity.

Let me make three important points right here.

KEEPING TIME
First, when you give your prospect the time the meeting will take, stick to it. If they want you to continue, by all means do so. But keep your integrity and honor theirs by saying 25 minutes and taking 25 minutes.

THEY'RE INTERESTED
The next point is that I assume that people are interested in the business opportunity as well as learning about the

products. If they're not, they'll tell you when you ask, "Is that fair?"

If they say no to the opportunity, you can focus your presentation on having them try the products (remember your company's money-back, satisfaction guarantee). You can bring up the opportunity at a later date after they've had time to experience benefits from your product or service. It's considered wise to leave an open door.

The third point is:

KIS&D

Which means: Keep It Simple and Duplicatable.

One of the greatest mistakes people in our business make is to assume they need to share all the information they know in one presentation. In fact, it's just the opposite that creates effective presentations. Remember, what we're doing here is saying the "right things to the right people." Less really is more.

The people with whom you talk to are going to make their decision on whether to become involved based on two things... "Is the product and opportunity of value for me, and can I see myself doing successfully with others, what they're doing with me?

Now, this second point is not really a conscious thing for most people. However, it's probably the most important point of all.

IT'S *NOT* ABOUT SELLING

Have you heard Network Marketers say that professional

sales people have a tough time in our business? That's not because they can't sell—it's because they *can!*

Do most people imagine that they could sell as well as a pro? Absolutely not. What's more, they don't want to! It's the same as imagining yourself as an expert. And the reason I say people respond to this subconsciously, is that most of us don't like to admit we're not sure we can do something.

So if your prospect thinks he or she is going to have to sell, or become an expert about the product or compensation plan, he or she will doubt that it's possible. They will create some excuse for not being interested. Yet, it's simply that they're uncomfortable seeing themselves as a salesperson or an expert.

So, K I S & D—Keeping It Simple and Duplicatable enables your prospect to put him or herself in your place, easily making effective presentations and being a successful Network Marketer.

One of the best ways of doing this, is by using a "Presentation Book."

YOUR PRESENTATION BOOK

A presentation book is a three-ring binder that's a composite of pictures, company literature, graphic illustrations, etc. It clearly communicates thousands of words (facts, figures and ideas) to your prospect about your products and business opportunity in an exciting and powerful way.

We've all heard a picture is worth a thousand words. But how often do we tend to use all those words when a picture would have been much more effective? And which is more duplicatable, teaching someone how to speak all those words, or showing them how to flip through a few pictures? Right.

What's more, making a presentation book is great fun.

PRESENTATION BOOK MEETINGS

I encourage people to hold presentation book meetings. Here's what you do.

Get everybody together—all your new people and some "seasoned pros" too. You can provide the materials or you can advise them what to bring. Three ring binders, those sticky papers they use in "magnetic" photo albums, three-hole punched plastic sleeves, colored poster board and paper, magic markers, scissors, some paper glue and a ton of magazines.

Start by having the experienced people show their books and tell everybody why they use this picture or that chart. Before you know it, people are shouting out new ideas and you've got a creative explosion on your hands.

Have people cut out headlines from articles and ads in magazines, pictures, charts and photos from company literature, newsletters and brochures. I've seen some utterly fantastic presentation books.

One of my students has one that begins on the first page with "The Great American Success Story," which she cut out of the jacket from the book of the same name. Another found an ad that had one of those pedestrian, cross-walk traffic signs in it that said "Don't Wait," and he uses it on the page where he had his company's business opportunity benefits pasted in from the compensation plan brochure.

Another woman shows her nutritional product on a page filled with pictures of happy, healthy looking people she cut out of magazine ads. Some people use this "press-on type" you can buy in art supply stores that makes really professional looking headlines.

The creative possibilities are endless. The meeting is fantastic fun—and generates tremendous enthusiasm and the people have real pride in their presentation books. Its great!

STEP NUMBER THREE: CREATE THE DESIRE

Now you begin to give them the information they need to *want* your product and opportunity.

Here's what you start with.

NETWORK MARKETING COMES FIRST

The first thing in your book, after your title page, should be something positive explaining the Network Marketing industry. With the assumption that most of the people you sit down with will be business opportunity prospects, this should be the first part of your presentation.

Now, there are three kinds of people you'll be making presentations to.

The smallest group will be people who know about and support Network Marketing. The next group will be people who don't know about it at all. And sadly, perhaps the largest group will be people who have pre-conceived beliefs, or outright negative experiences. You have already discovered where your prospect is by asking them what they knew about our business.

Ideally, we would like to have all the people we talk to understand, right up front, that Network Marketing is a legal and highly effective method of marketing. A proven and professional system of distribution that is currently America's fastest growing industry. A viable example of Free Enterprise at its purest level—simply because it allows everyone the Opportunity and the Freedom to own their own life and be the best that they can be.

So have examples in your Presentation Book of facts and features that convey these benefits to your prospect. Use graphic illustrations and high-integrity success stories of both individual and company accomplishments. Seek out credible publications and positive articles written on Network Marketing. The future is bright for our industry. The influx of mid-management and corporate America—plus Fortune 500 giants—is quickly bringing long-overdue attention and professionalism to our industry.

OUR INTERNATIONAL ASSOCIATION

Invest in its future while securing yours. Learn about our international trade association in Irvine, CA. USA—the Multi-level Marketing International Association (MLMIA). Its sole purpose is to promote and strengthen our industry throughout the world. They have valuable information, services and tools that can be of tremendous benefit to all of its individual and corporate members.

And whenever something negative happens in our

industry—investigate it! Refuse to let "hear-say" dictate your attitude and beliefs about this business. Whatever happens, both good and bad, there are always valid and/or legal reasons for it. Get the facts. Each time you do, you can't help but become a more knowledgeable and prepared professional. And remember, as Dr. Black put it so well..."Whatever the cause, multi-level companies fail, not because of the multi-level principle, but because people don't support the principle with honesty and excellence. So have faith in the multi-level principle and take care to be honest and accept only excellence."*

One other point: You may want to have a page in the back of your book you can turn to, if needed, that makes the distinction between an illegal pyramid scheme and a legitimate Network Marketing company. You can have two headlines with a brief definition beneath each one. Dr. Black's words in "Your Introduction" of this book will give you some good ideas for this.

IS THIS A PYRAMID SCHEME?

A pyramid scheme is an illegal lottery where participants are paid to recruit other people into the scheme. Network Marketing is *marketing* through a *network* of people.

Marketing means the movement of a product or a service from a manufacturer to the ultimate consumer. The only way people in Network Marketing earn money is on the movement of these goods and services. Network Marketers should never be paid a commission on people they sponsor.

---

* "The MLM Simple Success Guide" by K. Dean Black, Ph.D. (Brerie Enterprises, Springville, UT), p. 1-5.

This first part of your presentation book is very important. If you don't establish the credibility of Network Marketing *right away*, you may be giving an entire presentation to someone who's made up their mind to say no—no matter what you have to offer. This is why you asked them about their thoughts and feelings regarding being in business for themselves and Network Marketing early on in your presentation.

Addressing this up front creates the opening for the rest of your presentation. When you help them see how explosive and exciting our industry really is—that "opening" can get big enough to drive a truck through!

Another effective source of reference for you and your prospects is *Winning The Greatest Game of All—Network Marketing* by Randy Ward. Randy does an excellent job connecting people with the philosophy of our industry. He stresses the importance of contribution and service—the driving forces of Network Marketing. Everyone who reads this book will walk away with a greater appreciation for our people-helping-people industry.

THE COMPANY

The biggest question mark in your prospect's mind is, *"Is your company credible and professional?"* In a matter of two or three minutes, you can establish that credibility *and more* if you use the power of pictures.

For example: every good company has literature with pictures of the principles. It should contain a little bit about them and their experience, and a statement of the company's philosophy or mission. They'll probably also have a picture of the home office. Show that, too.

One great thing to do throughout your book is to use different color highlighter markers to make certain parts of the copy stand out. You can point to them and read them to your prospect at the same time, which really gets the message across.

If your company's been in business for a number of years, show a graph of their annual sales growth from year to year.

PUT YOURSELF IN THE PICTURE

Now, just imagine, you turn the page and there's a picture of you standing next to and shaking hands with the principles of your company. These men and women frequently participate at company events and trainings. The next time you're there, grab your camera and get a picture taken with them. It shows your prospect you're really serious—and well regarded by your company too. That's powerful stuff.

THE PRODUCTS

Remember to highlight the key benefits of the products or service in your book, point to them and tell your prospect about them.

This is the time to pull out your products. If they're great tasting, give your prospect a taste. Any Show-Tell-Taste-Touch-Smell you can give them is a big, big plus. Get their senses involved.

Don't hand them something to read. Throughout the entire process, keep them focused on you, your presentation book—and especially your products. Don't give them any distractions. You can give them brochures to take home later.

BENEFITS, BENEFITS, BENEFITS

It's very important that you focus on the product's benefits. Stay away from the facts and figures. Ninety-five percent of all the people you meet with want to know what the product *will do for them*. The best way to let them know this is to share what they've done for you and for others.

Last year 2.8 million 1/2 inch drill bits were sold in America. And every person who bought one *really wanted a 1/2 hole!* A product expert is impressive, but he or she is an imposing, intimidating figure that's hard to duplicate. So, K I S & D—Keep It Simple and Duplicatable.

THE PLAN

Next let's talk about your profit program or compensation plan. Here again, the most natural tendency is to give them too much detail. Don't!

Hit the high points. When you assemble your book, just put in the key features of your plan. Show them how and where they'll earn money, and where they can be one, two or three years from now.

I have the honor of working with thousands of Network Marketers throughout North America. Many of them are top performers in their company. It is my observation that 50 percent of them do not thoroughly understand their compensation plan—*and they could care less!*

The point is this. Give your prospects a graphic illustration of the plan and show them how to become a distributor. Explain the kit they'll be getting and what's in it. Show them all the benefits attached to owning their distributorship.

Avoid explaining things in detail, especially percentages, qualifiers and maintenance requirements. Tell them all of that is covered later in special training programs. Give them just enough information to make an informed choice. Remember, people just want to know...does the plan work? Not how it works! So have examples of distributor success stories that you can point to in your Presentation Book.

If you're presenting to a seasoned pro, he or she will ask you any specifics they want to know. If they do, give them the bottom line and move on.

SUPPORT AND TRAINING

The next part is to cover the support you and your company provide the people in your Network.

Here's where you want to identify all the events and training programs, what's going on locally in your area, and the sales support materials your company provides. Again, stay away from giving all the details.

Share how great the trainings are and how well the literature communicates the products and the compensation plan. Mention how great the people are and how much fun you're having. Also let them know how quickly you've learned the business and the kind of support and personal attention you're going to devote to them. Continually share your success and the success of others! It's the most contagious thing of all!

A great thing to do is to include pictures of your successful upline and sponsors. Again, include yourself in the pictures and let your prospect see how these successful people are open and supportive with you—and will be with your prospect as well. Let your prospect see how these people—who are just like them—are making the program work.

WHEN YOU CARE ENOUGH TO SEND...

And wouldn't it be great if a couple of days after your prospect joins, they get a call or a note in the mail. It's from one of these successful upline people pictured in your book, welcoming them into the Network and offering support. Wow! What a great first impression.

STEP NUMBER FOUR: OFFER THEM A CHOICE

At this point, your prospect is ready to make a decision. Here's where you explain to them what's available. You do that by giving them a choice. Present them with clear choices and put them in the picture.

"Bob, I think you can see why I'm so excited about this company, about these products and this opportunity. Tell me, if you were to get started here today how would you see yourself starting? Beginning to use the products and enjoying the benefits from them? Or, taking advantage of the business opportunity and starting that as well? Which of these two appeal most to you, Bob?"

If they can see themselves enjoying the products and experiencing the benefits for themselves first, great! Help them get started on the products and remind them of the 100 percent satisfaction guarantee.

If they can see what a wonderful opportunity this is and they're excited about building their own business, that's great! Find out which products they want now and make them a retail customer right then and there. Retail sales are important for a number of reasons.

First, a retail sale establishes a value for the product and it sets a pattern for how your prospects will approach doing the business themselves.

Retail sales and retail commissions pay you for the time you've invested in making the presentation. When everybody in your organization is making retail sales with their presentations, monthly sales volume and the commissions earned from them get bigger and bigger! It also helps your prospect see how retailing will generate immediate income for them too.

AN IMPORTANT POINT

And I can't stress this enough.

Do not fall into the trap of creating an instant wholesale customer.

The ability to purchase the products wholesale is a real benefit. If you allow this, your prospect will tend to do the same, and everybody in your organization will lose this fundamental income earning aspect of their business. Also, retail sales helps create even greater value for the distributorship itself. A lack of emphasis on retail sales is why so many distributors have organizations that don't reach their full potential.

I think it's one of the primary reasons for the high turnover of new distributors as well. Making presentations and retail sales *at the same time* is a real key for your new distributor's success. Explain that once he or she gets the application in, they'll be able to buy the products at wholesale. This also helps motivate your prospect to get the paperwork handled promptly. I suggest you help fill out the application right there and then offer to send it in.

STEP NUMBER FIVE: "YOU'VE MADE THE RIGHT CHOICE"

It's very important to assure your prospects, whether they've purchased your products or enrolled in your opportunity, that they've made the right choice.

Go back to the compliments you used in the very beginning and acknowledge how special they are, and how you'll stand by them to make certain their relationship with you and your company is a tremendous success.

It's also a great idea to follow up with a call or note.

Let me tell you a true story that will help you understand what I mean. There's this wonderful men's clothing store in San Diego. They have the greatest assortment of European casual clothes. I love clothes, and I love to shop. I don't know what possesses me, but everytime I go in there, I can't leave until it's $500 to $1500 later. Afterwards, I have time to think about what I've just done, and many times I question it. You know, the old buyer's remorse. Then, like timely clockwork, I get this wonderful card and note from Paul, the owner of the store, saying how nice it was to see me again. How much he appreciates me. How great I always look and how other people will notice my fashionable appearance. After reading his card and personal message, it never fails. I always go back to feeling good about my original decision.

Can you see how this professional and caring technique can help remove the buyer's remorse in your new customer or distributor's mind?

I CHALLENGE YOU TO BECOME A MASTER PRESENTER

I'd like to extend a personal challenge to you. I challenge you to become a master presenter. Here's how you do that. Tape record your presentations.

Tell your prospect that you want to perfect your presentation, and ask if they have any objection to you recording it. It's unlikely that anyone would object.

That tape recorder is also a marvelous tool for you. It lets your prospect know how serious you are, and they tend to take a more active and cooperative role in the presentation as well.

Now, once you've recorded your presentation, listen to it over and over again while your driving in your car or doing yard work. Look for ways you can improve your communication. See if there are any ways you could say things better.

One of the most important things to do is count how many questions you've asked your prospect. Always look for ways to ask more and more quality questions. Really study yourself and your presentation to discover new things you can do to improve it.

Do this with your first presentation for two weeks. Then, record your next presentation and compare the two. Repeat this cycle for 60 to 90 days and I promise you, at the end of that period, your presentations will be ten times better than when you started. And you'll have mastered the art of giving effective presentations.

Fair enough?

Now, in the next chapter, we'll talk more about the decision making process. We'll cover a method of asking and answering questions that will give you and your new distributors a powerful way to have all your prospects make the right choice for both of you.

Whew! Seems like a lot, doesn't it?

Well, your presentation can take as little as 20 or 25 minutes. Surprised? Don't be. The truth is, it takes a lot longer to *explain* a presentation that it does to *give* one.

So, are you as excited as I am with all of this? Can you see how empowering this is for your new distributors? This is powerful stuff! I can't wait until you read the next chapter.

It's all about Objections.

Chapter Seven: Objections

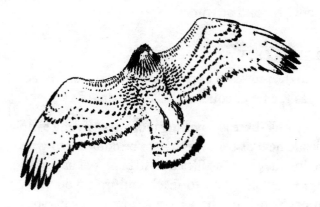

Now, let's see if we can sail through the Network Marketing maze of objections. "Objections" are what I refer to as "opportunities in work clothes." They're terrific possibilities to clear up misconceptions, remove resistance and diminish doubt. They really open up the relationship between you and your prospect for a positive outcome. Are you ready? Let's go!

One thing you should know about objections— they can come at any time. At the beginning, during or even after your presentation. When you're making appointments, at meetings, during follow-ups—anywhere and anytime.

BE A BOY SCOUT

The key to dealing with objections efficiently and effectively is, as the Boy Scouts say, "Be prepared."

I don't think there is anything more devastating to an enthusiastic new distributor than to be confronted with an objection they have no idea how to handle. That's why it's so important for you to teach and train your new distributors before they have to "go it alone." That's your responsibility as a Sponsor. And in fact, responsibility is part of what the word sponsor means.

TEAM TOGETHERNESS

It's a great idea to help your new distributors do their first couple of presentations. Allow them to go with you on some of yours, just to experience what it's like. We'll talk more about this in Chapter Eleven, "Duplication."

Have your new distributor explain to his or her prospect that they just started their business, and you, as their Sponsor, are there to train and support them as well as answer any questions. This "team" approach is an excellent way to train new people and assure they achieve initial retail sales and sponsoring success.

New distributors may feel shy about doing this, because they feel it conveys some sign of "weakness" to their prospect. But actually, the reverse is true. There's immediate respect for your honesty and integrity, and it puts the prospect in an attitude of pulling for you.

You see, people really want *you to succeed.* That's just natural. And it immediately sets a relaxed and open, understanding and receptive tone for the presentation. It also makes the Sponsor an expert. And you want that! It's been proven time and time again, preparation is the key to success in our business. This is especially true when dealing with so-called objections.

OPPORTUNITIES OR STUMBLING BLOCKS?

Objections are opportunities in work clothes.

To a brand new distributor, an objection is a stumbling block. To a seasoned Network Marketer, they are stepping stones. It's not "the challenge" to "overcome" that makes them so valuable. It's the *possibilities.* Almost all objections open up greater possibilities for understanding—and they're another perfect opportunity for you to transfer your enthusiasm and get your message across to your prospect.

I ask you to look at objections as nothing more than questions in disguise.

That's why I don't teach people "how to handle" or "overcome" objections. I just show them how to answer questions. When you "get" an objection, it means that your prospect simply doesn't yet have enough information to make an informed choice. *Objections have little, if anything, to do with personal rejection.*

Sometimes, objections are used to slow down the decision making process.

Again, the objection may stem from one or more unanswered questions. It may be a hidden question. Which means your job will be to uncover that and help your prospect reveal their true, underlying question, and then answer *that* for them.

SIX STEPS FOR SUCCESS

Anyone at all can use this process. It works in any industry, in any application. I know this, because ten years ago, before I switched careers into Network Marketing, I was in the medical industry—and these six steps worked perfectly there, too.

The core of this system is its comprehensive effectiveness. You can use it for discovering the question underlying the objection... bringing it to the surface without any emotional "charge"... and answering that question honestly and in such a way that your prospect both understands intellectually and feels emotionally secure as well.

Now, this doesn't mean that by using this process you will walk away from every single presentation with your prospect started on the product or service, or enrolled in the business opportunity.

What it *does* mean is that you truly can be complete with your prospect, and you will know you did your best in that situation. So no matter what their response, you're in a strong, winning position, and you've kept your momentum building towards greater success.

So, here are the six steps. And remember, an objection is only a question in disguise.

STEP #1: LISTEN LIKE YOU'VE NEVER LISTENED BEFORE

(You knew I was going to say this didn't you?) Put on your big ears and listen *carefully* to your prospects' questions. Bite your tongue if you have to, but don't interrupt your prospect or assume that you know what they're going to say.

Have you ever been in an interaction with someone where even before you finished what you were saying, they either finished your statement, or answered what they thought was your question? How's that feel? Even if they "guess" right, you feel "ripped off," don't you? It's very rude.

Let me tell you a story.

BILLY'S STORY

Back ten years ago in San Diego, I had a friend named Billy. He was one of the most likable guys you'd ever want to meet. We played on the same softball team. Billy was the kind of guy who had very little self-esteem. He was a carpenter—didn't really like his work, but he made decent money, so he kept at it.

One day after a game, we were having pizza and I was talking about the great time I just had while I was out with Lynn Diets, a dear friend of mine who lived and worked for me in Atlanta. Billy comes up to me and says, "Hey John, do you think the next time you go to Atlanta, I could go with you?"

I was floored. Billy had never gone anywhere before! He was so quiet and shy, and he didn't believe he could do anything really well—or even do anything different, for that matter. I was amazed he'd even asked.

So I said, "Billy, I'm going back in 46 days. Here are my flight times. If you buy a ticket on the same flight, we'll go to Atlanta together and once we get there, everything is on me." Now it was his turn to be floored! I'll never forget the look on his face.

For weeks, all Billy could talk about was going to Atlanta and finding one of those "Georgia Peaches."

We flew to Atlanta. Lynn picked us up at the airport and dropped us off at his house. He went out to conduct some business before we got together later to go out on the town. I thought this was a perfect opportunity to stroll down Peach Tree Lane and show Billy the sights.

So we're walking up and down Peach Tree Lane and I was showing Billy the governer's mansion, and this and that, when all of a sudden, Billy grabbed my arm and said, "John, did you see that, did you see that?" I said, "No, what, Billy?" and looked around. Billy said, "Boy, is she a peach!" So I told him, "Oh, yeah, I saw that," and we walked on.

A couple of minutes later, Billy grabbed me again. "John, did you see that, did you see that?" So I said, "No, what Billy?" He said, "Wow, was she a peach!"

Well, this happened a couple more times, and each time it was the same, "See, see... what a peach!" exchange.

Then Billy grabbed my arm again and said, "Did you

see that, did you see that?" And to tell you the truth, I was getting a little tired of this. So I said, "Yeah, yeah, Billy, I saw that,"—even though I hadn't—just to make him happy. And Billy looked at me with this weird expression and said,

"Then why did ya step in it?!"

After that, I never assumed I knew what anybody was going to say.

STEP #2: BE A DETECTIVE

Here's where you look beneath the objection's disguise for what your prospect is really asking.

For example: Let's say your prospect says, "Oh, yeah, this is like one of those pyramid things I've heard about." That's a pretty common objection. But what are they really asking? Now, most of us tend to get defensive at this point and take off on a defense of the entire industry. But they just want to know if this is legal.

The same thing with, "I just don't have the time to do this." Is there really a hidden question there? Such as, "Can I do this successfully with the limited time I have now?"

Here's your first clue: Objections come looking just like statements of fact—*when they are actually questions*. Here's what you can do easily to reveal those hidden questions. Add "Is that true?" to their statement, and then you can answer that question for your prospect.

The best way to do that begins with the next step.

STEP #3: AGREE AND APPRECIATE THE OBJECTION

...and ask for clarification if you need to.

Here's how it goes.

"Chris, I appreciate what you're saying." Now, notice something important here, I don't say "BUT" and then follow with a defense. Just appreciate what she's saying and stop for a moment. If *you* don't understand, or if you're not sure *she* really understands—ask.

"Chris, I'm not certain what you're saying here. Would you say that a little differently for me?" or "Chris, please say more about that."

By doing this you immediately put your prospect at ease. Now the conversation becomes an inquiry, with both of you sharing and being in search of what's best and true. That's a lot different than "overcoming an objection."

STEP #4: RESPOND

And do so by telling a story.

Stay away from a fact-packed, intellectual answer. No matter how good it is, or how right you are, you just squashed what they said, and when you do that, you squash *them* as well. However, when you tell a story— just as you do when explaining the benefits of your product—there's no threat and you appeal to them on an emotional level as well as on a rational level. And that's the best. Remember, your answers should make sense and satisfy their feelings as well.

Most of the objections in our business are quite common. When you learn the most common "objections," and answer them as questions in disguise, they merely become opportunities in work clothes. Before the end of this chapter, we'll go over a simple process of using an *Objection Worksheet* to help you and your people master this.

To respond to most objections (questions), I like to use the *feel, felt, and found* approach. For example, in response to the "time" question:

Acknowledge how they *feel* first. Then, create a real sense of kinship and trust by sharing how you've *felt* something similar. Then, tell them what you've *found* is how it really works, or happens, or is—*from your own experience.*

"Chris, I know just how you *feel.* Time is really valuable, isn't it? I *felt* that finding the time to do this was going to be a problem for me too. What I *found* to my surprise, though, was that this business is so flexible, that in the beginning, I could invest as little or as much time as I wanted. And you know what happened after just a couple of months? I was having such fun, and getting so much help, that I became more successful every week. So, I began investing more time in Network Marketing and because my now successful business is home-based, I have more time with my kids, I can play golf twice a week instead of only once, and... "

...and so it goes.

By the way—*never lie.* If you do, I promise you'll eventually get caught. The hardest work in the world is trying to remember which false story you told to whom. And having to continue it the next time you see that person is just awful. Besides, the truth—even a brief story that doesn't seem anywhere near as compelling as the one above—can still be powerfully persuasive. It works.

STEP #5: GET CONFIRMATION

Just as with travel arrangements in a foreign country, check out whether or not they heard and understood what you "think" you said.

"Does that make sense to you, Chris?" or "Do you see how that could happen for you?" or "Does that address your concern, Chris?"

Don't make assumptions. Remember Billy's story— you don't want to "step in it!" Get their agreement all along the way, and step #6 will be a "piece of cake."

STEP #6. GIVE THEM A CHOICE

...of things they can do to get started.

Now, you only do this last step if you've uncovered all the hidden questions they have. If you haven't, check it out with them, and if there are still doubts or "objections" remaining, go back up to Step #1 and take each objection or question one at a time through each of the steps. Repeat the entire process as many times as you have to to be certain it's decision making time.

When it is, *give them a choice.*

When your prospect agrees with your response (Step #5), it's only natural that a decision follows. Simply ask them a question (step #6) that brings your presentation full circle to the point of completion.

For example: If I had talked with Chris about her time

concern, and we'd gone through our *feel, felt and found* discussion ending up with her agreeing that what I said made sense, I could say to her:

"That's great, Chris. There are a couple of ways we could start out here. You could get some of the products to try. Use them for a couple of weeks and experience the benefits for yourself. And remember Chris, there's an unconditional satisfaction, money-back guarantee."

"Now, if you think there may be an exciting business opportunity for you here, then we can fill out your application right now. I'll help you get started—and remember, as soon as the company processes your application, you can begin ordering products directly and get the full wholesale discount. In the meantime, we can immediately get started building your business. So, Chris, which is the best way for you to start?"

It's vital that whenever you want your prospect to complete his or her decision—whether it's to purchase products, become a distributor or go with you for that first meeting—you give him or her a choice between two or more things to do. Use times, or days, or any two things to choose between.

CHOICE IS A GIFT

I want you to be really clear about one thing. *Giving your prospects a choice is a real service to them.*

The decision making process includes all the steps of your presentation: asking questions, sharing information and stories, discussing benefits, substantiating them with features, etc. The final step is giving them *the choice.* That's when they have to make a decision.

Making a decision is often hard for some people, because if you don't offer them a choice, they still see it as the whole big decision, which is a much more involved and complex process.

But a choice is simple. It's between this one or that one. By asking them what they choose to do, you help them focus on one or the other. And you encourage them to choose between two positive choices. If you've received their confirmation all along, then the choice is whether to invest in the products or become a distributor—or both. So when you get to the final step of offering the choices, it's not yes or no—it's simply *yes*. It's now just a matter of your prospect choosing *which* yes!

WHAT ABOUT ANOTHER OBJECTION?

Treat it just like the first, or the third, or the fifth. Go back to Step #1 and continue through Step #6 until you come out of the process with a "yes" or a "no."

WHAT ABOUT "NO?"

A "yes" to me is anytime they don't say "no."

Now, if they're still throwing objections at me—that's different. Those are questions, not answers. A "no" is a direct answer. And I honor a "no"—no matter how much I may personally disagree with it.

"I'm not interested." "This just isn't right for me." "I wish you the best, but it's not what I want to do."

Those are solid "no's." What do you do then? Accept the "no" for what it is. Thank them. Keep the door open—*and move on to the next "yes!"*

Although we've used the example of a presentation here, these six steps are applicable to any situation such as setting an appointment or following through.

AN OBJECTION WORKSHEET

A good idea to help you teach others in your Organization about objections, is to have an objection worksheet. (An example is in Chapter Ten)

You can have them printed up listing the most common objections you and your people encounter. You can even use creative brainstorming to have everyone generate objections. Then go back over each objection in a role-playing exercise. Have individuals or teams find the underlying questions and go through the six-step process. Then ask different people to share how they answered each objection.

Ninety to ninety-five percent of all the "objections" you get are the same ones that have been answered again, and again by hundreds, even thousands of distributors. You may have one or two that are unique to your product or opportunity, but for the most part they're the same old questions.

Again, preparation is the key to success. That's why your training should include an objection worksheet and a session on how to answer the underlying questions. Remember that famous line, "An ounce of prevention (i.e., preparation) is worth a pound of cure."

PREPARATION VERSUS REJECTION

The feeling of personal rejection is the most devastating

part of our business. And what upsets me most is—*it's so unnecessary!*

Would you be willing to be with me on the outcome of a contest between Preparation and Rejection? I'd wager everything on Preparation. Why? Because that's what's worked for me—*time after time after time.*

No matter what aspect of Network Marketing we're discussing or exploring, the key to success is proper preparation. Turning an objection into a request for more information and discovering the hidden question is a sure-fire way to be prepared.

Herman and Hillary Hope-It-Happens prepare by building up their hopes. Al and Alice Achievers prepare by learning the proven principles of success, and then practicing them over and over until they master them.

NETWORK BRAINSTORMING CAN CREATE MASTER TRAINERS

Brainstorming is a wonderful way to *inform, involve* and *inspire* the men and women in your Network Organization. You can accomplish a powerful training session on objections as well as a number of other similar issues.

Here's how it works.

TAKE A TRAINING

Whether you're dealing with a small, intimate in-home gathering or a full-blown training session in a downtown hotel, you can create instant excitement, generate lots of creative energy and accomplish a high level of pro-active learning with *Brainstorming*.

Let's use the subject of "answering objections."

The training leader sets the stage. He or she explains the task at hand and the ground rules. In this instance, the object is to come up with objections—as many as possible. And there's really only one ground rule—there's no such thing as a "bad objection." Everybody gets to be right and every contribution gets written on the flip charts in the front of the room.

Leader says, "Okay, now call out the toughest objection you've ever gotten or that you can think of." And the training leader can continue to lure the group on by clarifying what he or she wants next. For example: "Great, now give me the dumbest objection you've ever heard... Now the most melodramatic... Now, the funniest..." etc.

When a flip chart page is full, tear it off, tape it up on the wall in plain sight of everyone and keep going on to the next one.

Just before you (the leader) sense the energy on this topic winding down, stop. Tell people not to write any of these down—they'll do that later.

PICK THE TOP TEN

Now, ask everybody to select five or ten of the most common objections on the charts. Try to get about ten of them. The leader then writes these ten down on a new sheet of paper on the flip pad, leaving several inches of space between each for notations. Have each student write them also on their "Objection Worksheet." (Copy the format of the Objection Worksheet in Chapter Ten.)

Now go through them, one by one, and have the group discuss what is the underlying question for each objection. Be sure to keep them focused and lead them through each one. When you arrive at a consensus, write down the underlying question directly beneath the objection. Have the students do the same on their worksheets.

When you're through with the top ten, ask the group if there are any others on the original charts that are especially difficult for them. If time permits, deal with those as well.

ANSWER THE QUESTIONS

Once the underlying question to each of these top objections has been determined—have the group answer them.

To do this, you can have a brainstorming session and involve the group as a whole. Or, you can set up teams of three to five people each, and have them answer the questions in smaller groups. You can also split everybody up into partners and have the pairs ask and answer each of the questions.

When you use teams or pairs, it's good to bring the whole group back together afterwards and have a select number of people share those answers they think are really excellent.

Also, check with the group to see how they experienced the exercise itself. When you do that, you give them all a chance to deepen their experience of working together, and people will really get into acknowledging each other as well. It's wonderful!

SO, WHAT HAVE YOU DONE?

1. You've networked!—and you'll feel the tangible throb of creative energy in the room. It *never* fails.

2. All of the people (there may be one or two hold-outs in a big room, but not many) have a real sense of ownership of the Objection Worksheet—because they made it themselves.

3. The concept has been driven home, because *they thought of it!* That's a lot different than someone else standing up there and telling them what to do.

4. They're *informed* (the objections, questions and answers on the worksheet itself), *involved* (the process lets them all play) and *inspired* (they've seen one great example of how powerful, creative and fun their Network can be).

5. And of course, any relatively new, enthusiastic, high energy distributor can lead this exercise. It's another example of people learning to master their subject, while teaching it to others. And, that's what *Being The Best You Can Be In MLM* is all about.

How else can you use Network Brainstorming in your Network Organization? Why don't you get your people together for a meeting to brainstorm *that* question?

Next chapter: let's Follow Through.

Chapter Eight:
Follow Through

Can you imagine what success golfers, tennis or baseball players would have if they stopped their swing as soon as they made contact with the ball? Not much. They would have no power, no ability to go the distance—even the direction of the ball would suffer. That's just what happens to Network Marketers who don't "Follow Through." This chapter will place in your hands one more key to mastery of your business— a proven, practical method for following through.

R emember Herman and Hillary Hope-It-Happens? Let me tell you about something they do all the time.

They invest a fair amount of time, energy and even money, locating their prospects. And they get a good number of these people started on their product or using their service. They even realize some initial success helping their prospects begin the business. Then they settle back and wait for those people to take off like rockets to success!

But they don't take off. Why?

GETTING DOWN (OR UP) TO BUSINESS

I believe with all my heart that once your prospect has joined, sent in a distributor application and started on the product—*that's the time you roll up your sleeves and go to work!*

Herman and Hillary seem to think that they've already finished the job. Now it's time for them to sit back, "Hope-It-Happens," and get ready for that first, fat bonus check.

That's not the way Network Marketing success works. And the operative word here is "works."

FOLLOW THROUGH

I've said before that one fundamental key to Network Marketing success is enthusiasm—remember the last four letters: I - A - S - M stand for I Am Sold Myself.

Perhaps the Hope-It-Happens feel that because they are so enthusiastic about their product and plan, everybody else will be, too. You know how it goes, "This is so great—*it will sell itself*."

Well, that doesn't happen. It takes work. And the specific kind of work it takes is—*follow through*.

About two years ago, I researched Fortune 500 companies to discover what they considered to be the most worthwhile investment of their resources, time, money and talent. What do you think it was? Research and development, advertising, sales, motivation...? It was...

CUSTOMER SERVICE AND SATISFACTION

These highly successful, multi-billion dollar businesses have realized that once they have made the sale, that's when their real work begins.

You see, making a sale is just that—making a *single solitary sale*. No business succeeds doing that.

Now, making *and keeping* a satisfied customer—one who comes back again and again, and one who enthusiastically recommends your product or service to others because he or she feels completely satisfied—now *that's* the way to build a successful business. And this is especially true in Network Marketing, where your satisfied customer becomes your productive distributor.

Again, the key is follow through.

A SIMPLE SYSTEM FOR SUCCESS

What I'm going to suggest now is a very simple and highly effective follow through system you can use to make success in your business *inevitable*.

Let me share one interesting point before I tell you the system.

Would you like to know one common thing I've found with *every* successful company and distributor in this business? It's this—*they all use the system I'm about to explain to you!* It's true. Sure, they've all got their own unique variations, special little ways they do this or that, but the essence of the system is the same. Here it is:

PICTURE THIS

I ask you to picture all of this in your mind as I tell it to you. Imagine yourself going to the office supply or stationary store. Select a 3 x 5 card file box in whatever color you like best. Pick one small enough to carry with you wherever you go.

Now, get a couple of packs of blank 3 x 5 cards. The ones with lines on them are best. Get some index card dividers with little tabs on them as well. Get two sets: one numbered one through 31 for the days of the month, and another with each of the 12 months of the year.

Now then, every time you have someone start on your product or your service, regardless of whether they're a retail customer or a distributor, fill out a 3 x 5 card on them. Write down their name, address and phone numbers at home and at work (if it's okay to reach them there). Also include anything unique and special about them: their spouse's name, kid's names too, any special interest they may have, or some part of their background that catches your attention. List it all down on their card.

Make a section on the card for what you've learned they want or like most about your product or opportunity. Keep it short and to the point. Just get all the relevant information that's useful for you to know about this person.

WHO KNOWS WHAT TO EXPECT?

As a distributor, you should be very familiar with what people normally experience when they begin to use your product or service. If you're just starting out, this is very important for you to know, so have your sponsor help you learn what to expect.

For example, if you're dealing with a nutritional product, or a weight-loss program, most of your customers will begin to experience benefits from using the products in a matter of a few days. The purpose here is for you to follow-up with them just at the time when they are beginning to feel the difference your products make.

You'll experience a number of immediate benefits from doing this.

First, your customers feel great knowing you're personally interested in how they're doing. They'll know how much you care—and that goes a long way in everybody's book.

What's more, it's a fact that both positive and negative experiences occur in people's minds. If you show concern and appreciation for your customers in the very beginning, you set the stage for all their positive expectations to be fulfilled. It gives your product a great head start.

USING YOUR FOLLOW-UP SYSTEM

Let's say today is the 19th of the month and just this

afternoon you got Mary started on the product. You know from experience that most people start to feel the benefits in about three days. So, on the 19th, after you have filled out Mary's card, place it back in the box behind the numbered tab for 22—the date three days from today.

Now, on the morning of the 22nd, the first thing you do when you get to your desk is open up your box and pull out all the cards behind the number 22.

Voilá—a business manager in a box.

So, you pick up the telephone, dial Mary's number (listed right there on the card) and ask, "How are you?" You'll learn one of two things right away: either Mary hasn't started using the product yet, or she has. Now, if she hasn't started using the product, you can encourage her to do that. Build up those positive expectations.

"Mary, I can't wait 'til you try this. Boy, are you gonna feel great!"

You can suggest different ways to use the product, try connecting it to some benefit or aspect of her life she really cares about, and you've got that written down in the information section of her card.

If she's begun to use the product, her answer to "How are you?" will tell you that, too. If that's the case, check out how she's doing with...

BENEFITS, BENEFITS, BENEFITS!

Now, if she hasn't realized any benefit yet, this is the time when you want to give her a benefit to look forward to. Don't give her all the technical information about the product. Share a story—your own or someone else's—

that's right for her and that will excite her about what she can expect.

"Mary, I know how interested you are in such and such (you get this 'inside info' right off the 3 x 5 card). Well, my friend Sharon, who's also into such and such, started using the product two weeks ago, and she told me yesterday that..."

You fill in that sentence with a true story of someone who's getting similar results to those Mary would like, and preferably someone to whom Mary can personally relate. For instance: someone who also loves to garden, as Mary does, is now spending an additional couple of hours gardening, simply because she feels great and has so much more energy.

If it's a service such as a discount telephone program for business use, you could tell how so and so is making more sales now. She no longer feels inhibited about making calls she needs to make, because they were just too expensive with her old phone company.

You've got the idea. Relate your story to both the lifestyle and the specific benefits for your customer.

WHAT ABOUT NEGATIVE RESPONSES?

Sometimes, when people first begin to use a health-changing product, they actually begin to feel *worse* before they start to feel better.

This is common and quite easy to explain; however, your customer may be genuinely alarmed or even tempted to stop using the product unless you're there to help. If your follow through call comes at the right time, you can ease your customer's mind by explaining how his or her body is cleansing itself of unwanted substances, and help them understand what's happening to them—so they feel more secure.

FOLLOWING THE OPPORTUNITY THROUGH

Now, this works just as well when the subject is the business opportunity itself.

When you call to find out how your new distributor is doing, you'll learn if they've started, what they're doing, if there are problems, etc., and you can use your 3 x 5 file here, too.

Perhaps you need to re-focus your distributor on his or her goals. If you've got them written down on that person's card, it's easy to do. Just as with a product, don't get into the technical aspects of the plan. Use stories and share personal experiences to illustrate your points.

"You know Mary, I had the same thing happen when I began. Here's what my sponsor shared with me, and boy, did that make a difference."

In this instance, as in the others, don't get technical—just share your experience.

The first few days and weeks are a vulnerable time for both customers and new distributors. Unfortunately, not everyone with whom they come in contact is going to be supportive of what they're doing. If you make the time to follow through with them, to support them and let them know you're there and you care, it can make all the difference in the world. Can you see how powerful follow-up calls can be?

How long is too long for your follow through calls? Monthly is too long.

How short is too short? Less than a couple of days is too little time for retail follow-up calls. It does depend on the nature of your unique product or service, but follow-up calls are best when made every three days to a week.

What about follow through calls to your new, serious distributors?

I suggest daily!

I've tried a number of different ways of doing this, and found that being in touch every day is the best and most productive. It allows you to coach people, support them in keeping their agreements and deal with their concerns before they become problems. It also helps them create new opportunities.

One of the best ways to recognize how serious your new distributor is, is by whether or not *they* call *you*. In fact, you may want to get an agreement from *them* to *call you* every day.

COLLECT *EVERY* STORY YOU HEAR

How do you come up with the *right* story at the *right* time for the *right* customer or new distributor?

From your very first day in the business (or from right now, if you haven't already begun), you build what I call a Story Box. You can make it a part of your existing 3 x 5 card box or create a new one.

Your Story Box is a collection of all the stories you hear

at meetings and from other distributors about your products and opportunity.

Get into the habit of being at every function, attending every meeting you can. Approach people with a warm smile and friendly handshake. Introduce yourself, ask them about their experiences and listen intently to their stories. Ask their names, what they do for a living, who introduced them to the product or opportunity, what they're using, what benefits they're experiencing and so on. Every time you go to one of these functions, you should walk out with at least three to six new stories for your story box.

Try not to be too critical as to the "quality" or "interest" you feel the story has. A story that may not personally interest you could be perfect for someone else.

Index all these stories based on a one-or-two word description of the main benefit in the story and/or the kind of person it's about. You won't believe how quickly—and effortlessly—you'll fill your Story Box with wonderful, inspirational stories. You can never have enough of them.

And if you ever do get more than you can handle—send them to me. I love them. I never get enough great stories!

BECOME A MASTER STORY TELLER

Please, don't try to become a product expert. Don't try to become a marketing plan expert, either. If you want to be an expert, become an expert at getting and telling stories.

Do you know who the most successful Network

Marketers in the world are? They are master story tellers. The greatest salespeople, the greatest teachers, the most inspirational leaders, are master story tellers. And what's so beautiful is—story telling is easily duplicatable! Every one of us has been listening to and telling stories *all our lives!*

Remember, 95 percent of the time, people don't care about "the facts." The five percent who do care about the facts will ask you fact-finding questions straight out. When they do, give them what they want. And remember, even these people want to know what the benefits are and what the product or opportunity will do for them.

And what's the best way in the world to communicate benefits? That's right: tell a story.

FOLLOW-UP WITH FOLLOW THROUGH

With each follow-up call, get the person's agreement to get back in touch in a couple of days to find out how they're doing—and be sure to write the appointment down.

"Mary, I'm glad you're doing so well. That's fantastic! Will it be okay with you if I check back in two or three days, say Friday or Saturday?—which day would be best?"

Remember, it's best to give her the choice of when— and that's a very good way to have her not be thinking about "if."

When you get off the phone, write the results of your conversation on Mary's card—especially write a note

about the story you told her—and place the card behind
the tab for the 25th or 26th, as you both agreed.

When the 25th (or 26th) rolls around, you've probably got three or four cards with names of people to
follow-up with. That should take you 20 or 30 minutes,
45 at the most. Disipline yourself to follow through with
each of them. Within a couple of weeks, it will become an
empowering habit. And believe me, this is some of the
most productive time you will ever devote to your business.

So, you call Mary and start the same way, "How are
you?" If she *still* hasn't experienced some clear and tangible benefits from using the product (service or opportunity), what do you do?

Tell her *another* story. Talk about someone else this
time. And keep doing this—calling and telling another
story—until one of two things happens. Either she gets
completely discouraged and says, "I quit." because she
doesn't experience any benefits, or *she tells you a success
story!*

THE SPARK OF OPPORTUNITY

Mary's success story comes from a personal belief system
based on her having a direct experience of value with the
product or opportunity. This belief acts like a spark or
flame of desire for her to want to know more. That spark
is something you can work with and gradually build into
a bonfire! And you know what else? You've got another
great story for your Story Box.

With this follow through system, you're setting yourself
apart and above just about everybody else out there who's
selling anything! Really—think about it.

What happened *after* the last time you bought something; a car, new furniture, clothes, food, anything.

Did anybody call you up and say "How are you— how's that car, that couch, those cookies... working out for you?" Not many I bet. Those few who did, probably made you feel special—and you probably thought they were special too.

Follow through is very powerful stuff! When you follow through you're taking a stand for your product, your customer or your new distributor. You are on record as caring, concerned and committed.

My friends, do you know what that makes you? That makes you one in a million. And in time, it can make you a Millionaire In Motion as well.

Powerful? You bet!

ARE YOU A NUTRITION EXPERT?

I'd like to share with you a portion of an article I wrote for MLM Success™, a training publication in our industry for which I have a tremendous amount of respect. It's an important point, and it talks about a trap that many people in our business can't seem to help but fall into.

So many Network Marketing companies offer nutritional products. One thing I've witnessed far too often is the tendency many distributors have to want to become nutrition experts.

It's a natural thing, really. You begin using a product that changes your life for the better, and your innate curiosity causes you to want to know more.

How does this product work? Why does the body respond

this way or that? How do we know when we're really healthy—or not healthy, for that matter? How did we get in this condition in the first place? What are the individual ingredients in the product, and what do they do? Where do they come from? How are they made? How much is too much to take? What's the "active" ingredient? What's the nutritional breakdown of the product? Are there other products that do similar things? What kind of scientific research exists about the product? Which independent laboratory tested the product?

... and on and on and on.

Did you know that nutritional science is one of the youngest branches of scientific study? Think back for a moment. How long ago was it that you first heard about trace minerals, fiber, or cholesterol? Five years...ten years? Not much more than that, I bet.

The truth is nutritional experts, Ph.D.s and others, who've devoted their lives to the link between diet and health, are discovering new marvels and unveiling new information almost every day. Many times these new revelations are proving previous facts or opinions about nutrition to be untrue.

So I guess you could say that nutritional knowledge for now is a matter of opinion. And everyone is entitled to their opinion. By talking nutrition to your prospect, you can open the door to a "possible debate" instead of a simple "transfer of enthusiasm."

The challenge we have with acquiring more and more knowledge about nutrition is, "once enough of it goes in our ears and eyes, it starts coming out our mouth." The more "so called facts" we have the more "so called facts" we talk about. And that's *not* what makes people interested in, or want to try, any product—especially a nutritional one.

Futhermore—having a fistful of facts is like being the fastest gun in the West. There's always somebody faster—*always* somebody with more facts. If you try to establish your product or opportunity based on "the facts," sooner or later, someone will come along with more or better facts than you.

By all means, educate yourself. You will naturally expand both your desire for and exposure to greater and greater knowledge and awareness of nutrition and health. Perhaps the most important point is to allow others the "space" to let this natural desire grow at its own pace. That way, their enthusiasm remains intact and isn't replaced by an over-emphasis on facts and figures.

Marketing is made up of features and benefits. Features support benefits. People don't buy features, they buy benefits. They want to know what the product *will do for them*.

Besides, which is easier to *share*, the features or the benefits? And which is easier to duplicate?

"Tell the story." That's what the successful Network Marketers mean when they say, "The more you tell—the more you sell."

Next chapter—let's go to a meeting.

Chapter Nine:
The Opportunity
Showcase

Let's go to a meeting... a BIG meeting. That's what an Opportunity Showcase is, and what it does, is supercharge the engine of your business. The Opportunity Showcase acts like a transformer that dramatically boosts the energy of success for everybody involved: you, your prospects, new distributors and "seasoned pros" alike. Here's what the Opportunity Showcase is all about.

Have you ever been on an airplane and noticed how the coach passengers strain to get a look at what's happening up in first class? I get a big kick out of watching people do that. The grass up there is greener. First class is special.

GOING FIRST CLASS

First class in your Network Marketing business is your "Opportunity Showcase." That's the big once-a-week, bi-monthly or once-a-month meeting where everybody shows up looking great, sounding even *better*—and sharing their success with everyone else.

Opportunity Showcases can include all the Networkers from your company in your immediate area. It doesn't matter if there are a number of different downline organizations involved. The more the better. Fifty people is okay. One hundred or more is great! Synergy creates and sustains momentum and I'll talk more about the power of synergy before the end of this chapter.

Attending an Opportunity Showcase is like being part of an exclusive club. It's special. Just like first class.

Now that you've had your "belly-button to belly-button" presentation in your prospect's home or at a coffee shop, I'm sure they've started on your product or service. And I'm equally sure you show them how much you care by doing your proper follow-up. Now, because of the benefits they are starting to enjoy, they may be a little curious about the business. So it's time to expand their small and limited picture and show them the bigger picture. Your "first class" opportunity. That's what the Opportunity Showcase is all about.

WHY AN OPPORTUNITY SHOWCASE?

Let me address one question right up front. Are Opportunity Showcases necessary? I say "Yes." Why? Because they work! But it is the special way they work and what they accomplish that makes them so very powerful.

I've observed companies that use the concept of the Opportunity Showcase and others that don't. The ones that do seem to be much more successful and grow faster, by far. A great Opportunity Showcase adds an inspiring and empowering dimension to your business and it adds it when it matters most—*at the beginning.*

Although this chapter deals with the physical form of the Opportunity Showcase in a very traditional manner (hotel, staff, registration, the works), don't get stuck in that form. For instance, there are new technologies today that enable Network Marketing companies and distributors to take all the elements of a great Opportunity Showcase and do them over the phone!

Conference calling is an excellent example. One call I listened to recently blew me away!

A friend gave me a number and told me to call. At the specified time, I did just that. An operator greeted me and told me to relax and enjoy the music—the call would begin in two minutes.

Now in all honesty, I can't stand that music. The rest of the call was superb and exciting, but that music has got to go! I'd rather hear information about the company or even better, a great talk about this exciting industry, but that elevator music...

At any rate, in a couple of minutes just like the man promised, I heard the following:

"Hi, welcome to the XYZ Opportunity Showcase. I'm so excited about this product and the fantastic opportunity we've got here. It's great that you're going to invest a few minutes with us and learn for yourself just what this super opportunity is all about. In all my years in Network Marketing, I've never experienced anything like it!"

"Hey, do you know how many people are on the call tonight? Over one thousand people, from all across the United States and Canada! Isn't this great? Let's go!"

"Bob, in San Diego, are you there?" "Hi, John, I'm right here and rarin' to go!"

"Sally, in Florida, are you on the line?" "Sure am, John, it's great to be here again."

"David in New York—are you with us?" "Hey, John, how are you tonight?"

And so it went...

There were five people who interacted on the call, plus the company president. Each was a new distributor who'd been in the business for only a couple of months. And they conducted the call almost exactly like the format I'll be teaching you for the Opportunity Showcase in this chapter. It was amazing!

They covered all the bases—answered all the fundamental questions. They conveyed an image of explosive growth, excitement and enthusiasm for the products, the company and the opportunity. People told their stories and it was full of emotion, information and inspiration. It was great! I was really impressed!

There were 1000 people, sitting comfortably at home in their own chairs and couches all throughout North America—all taking part in an Opportunity Showcase. There were groups of distributors gathered around speaker phones, too. They listened to the 25 minute call and then held a smaller follow-up meeting of their own.

John Naisbitt was right—high-tech *and* high-touch. The future is here today.

My point is: the structure of the Opportunity Showcase can be done in a variety of ways. I'm going to explain it to you as if it were a classic meeting in a hotel—but throughout my description, please understand that you can use the principles and apply them any way you like.

Now, let's talk some more about what the Showcase can do.

ENTHUSIASM AND DOUBT

What does the person who's just started enjoying the benefits of the product or service have in common with the brand new distributor?

1) Raw enthusiasm, and
2) The required "dose of doubt" that we all have when we start something. It's natural.

Bill tells me, "John, I'm so excited about these products and this business."

I say, "Bill, you're going to do just great." Bill thinks, "But... What if.... Can I...?" etc.

An Opportunity Showcase can blast right through those initial doubts.

I'm real big on "sure-start" programs, and I've never found a better way to make a solid, powerful beginning for new distributors than a well-done Showcase. And for the prospect who still has a "coach class mentality" about your opportunity, the Showcase can expand that picture to "first class."

WHO IS AN OPPORTUNITY SHOWCASE FOR?

The Showcase is for the benefit of *everyone's* prospects—and new distributors too! It's okay if the Showcase is the very first contact a prospect has with the product and opportunity.

Although everybody benefits by being there, the purpose is to give your guests (prospects and new distributors) a great, first-class look at this fantastic business. The Showcase is their formal introduction to the company and the network.

They'll meet other new people just like themselves who are starting out in the business. They'll meet seasoned, successful distributors, learn more about the company and all it has to offer. Most importantly, they'll get first hand, direct experience with the exciting, powerful, professional organization they should and could be getting involved with.

OPPORTUNITY SHOWCASES PROVIDE A CONTEXT

That's why they're so perfect for your business prospects. They "show and tell" your people that all those possibilities you told them about in your presentation are very real indeed.

The company is real. The products and services are real and they really work. And there are dozens, even hundreds or thousands of *real* men and women just like them who are out there doing the business successfully. They know it's true, because they're meeting many of them in person at the Opportunity Showcase.

And the Showcase makes one more thing very real—the knowledge that they don't have to do it alone! And believe me, that's one of the biggest doubts every prospect and new distributor has. When they look around that room and see all those successful people and all the new people coming on board, they not only know it's possible to succeed in this business—they can't wait to get started!

It's interesting, but people coming into Network Marketing have two conflicting desires. They want to get in early—you know, "be the first kid on their block." Yet, they want a "sure thing"—one that other people have already proven works. A good Opportunity Showcase contains all the enthusiasm of an explosive "ground floor" opportunity and the security of joining something lots of people are already doing successfully.

THE ELEMENTS OF A GOOD SHOWCASE

An Opportunity Showcase is truly a work of art. Each one is unique to you and your product and your company.

Opportunity Showcases are real Networking efforts. All the distributors and leaders come together in a given area to put them on. Since they benefit everyone in the entire Network, they're a matter of cooperation—not competition. There's no concern about who's in whose organization or downline. It's a family affair.

The various behind-the-scene jobs that putting on a Showcase requires are shared by all the Distributor Networks in the area. I suggest these responsibilities be delegated by the sales leaders on a revolving basis. That way, every group gets to participate and contribute to the different parts of the Opportunity Showcase. This also helps everyone train their people better. I'll explain what each of these functions are throughout this chapter.

Here are some basic ingredients every Opportunity Showcase should contain.

A FIRST-CLASS LOCATION

First, the Showcase takes place in a hotel or recognized "business" function facility. Opportunity Showcases should not be done in homes, garages or spare rooms of any kind. Occasionally, a church function room can work. The key here is that the location *must* immediately convey a sense of prosperity and success.

Remember, we're going first-class here. A recognized, well-thought-of location, with well-lit parking in a good neighborhood, is strongly advised.

If the hotel is a big one, have a person greet your guests in the lobby and show them how to get to the room. Don't rely on signs or the hotel marquée. I'm sure there are worse things than wandering lost in a hotel looking for a meeting room—but not many. If you need to station people along the path to the room to show the way, do that, too.

REGISTRATION

Next is a registration area with a registration table. It's best if this is set up outside the meeting room itself. Sometimes that's not possible, but I think it's the best way.

The registration area is where you'll "formally" greet your guests, so staff the registration table with the most friendly, cordial people in your Network. Pick the men and women with the biggest smiles and most pleasing personalities. Just remember the power of first impressions. Put the people there that you'd like to have your guests meet first.

NAME TAGS ARE A MUST

Many people do not remember names well. Having name tags takes the burden off each guest's memory and lets him or her relax.

I suggest name tags with different colored borders. That way your guests can all have one color and the "seasoned pros" will have another.

Let people know what the color scheme means when you're filling in their name tag. That way they can feel comfortable about approaching the right people if they have a question or something they want to say.

A system of different colored tags also helps experienced distributors to introduce themselves to your guests. And having five or six people come up to you and say, "Hi, my name's so and so, it's great to have you here," makes people feel welcome, relaxed, and very positive.

MEET EVERYONE YOU CAN

Make it a policy at Showcases to talk with *every* guest. Find out how she or he came to be there. Learn what products they've tried and how they like them. Have them talk about what they hope to get out of the business. Not only does this warm up the guests, but it's a great learning opportunity for you and usually adds to your Story Box as well.

SIGHTS AND SOUNDS

I believe in having music at Opportunity Showcases— even at trainings for that matter. It sets a great tone—no pun intended—and really empowers your events.

Play something upbeat and lively. Don't use anything exotic or weird. Pick music that moves people and will make them want to come into the room. Music that's uplifting, positive and hopeful. Don't have it too loud, but it's good if the music causes people to speak up a bit.

I was in Toronto, Canada, doing a seminar and a few of the sales leaders took me up to this great restaurant that has a 360° view of the city. It was mid-afternoon and although there were a number of people in the restaurant, it was ghostly quiet.

I didn't notice at the time, but we were very low-key ourselves. You know, hushed voices, relaxed, low energy.

All of a sudden, I noticed people standing up, moving around, the voices had gotten louder. Our group was more animated, too. The entire energy in the room was transformed. I was beginning to wonder if they had put something strange in our wine, when our waitress came over and I asked her what had happened.

She said, "Oh, they turned the music on. That always happens as soon as the music goes on."

A PRODUCT DISPLAY

Have a great product display in the back of the room.

Pick a couple of your distributors who are especially creative and let them design and build it. I'm not talking about a couple of bottles set up on a table. I'm talking about a great looking display! Like a still-life painting.

There are lots of little, inexpensive things you can do to make a terrific looking product display table.

Risers are blocks of wood or fabric-covered cardboard that allow you to have products sitting on the table at different height levels. You can purchase inexpensive frames or small, tabletop easels to show different company literature, quotes from satisfied customers, charts or graphs that are interesting, etc.

You can use props, too. For a nutritional product, you could have some of the ingredients there, such as stalks of wheat, fresh fruit, etc. For a diet product, before and after pictures, a tape measure and a bathroom scale.

Use your imagination and make it look really special. The attention put into your product display will pay off in many ways. A high perceived value for the product and a group of people who hold the products in high esteem are just two ways.

CHAIRS—LESS IS MORE

First, do your best to get confirmation from everyone who's coming and have them let you know how many guests they're bringing. Put out less chairs than you expect people to fill them. Have extra chairs stacked neatly in the back and have someone responsible for adding more chairs as new people come in.

Empty chairs have people thinking the meeting is poorly attended—no matter how many people actually are there. Constantly adding more chairs has them thinking, "Wow, this is really hot!"

IT'S SHOW TIME!

First, start and end on time. Doing this is professional. It supports all your people in keeping their time agreements, and shows respect for all the guests who made the successful effort to get there on time. I suggest 45 minutes as the best time for the formal part of the Showcase. The mind can only absorb what the bottom can endure. No longer than one hour, max!

However, a lot can be accomplished before and after the formal part of your Opportunity Showcase. Remember, when I told you to talk to as many people as possible before the Showcase? By doing this, you warm up your guests and build positive expectations for both the speakers and the meeting itself. After the Showcase, let your guests know that people will be available for questions and for sharing how they're doing in the business. This is also a great time for people to get better acquainted and for your prospects to complete their applications, purchase their products, or register for training.

THE FIRST SPEAKER

Pick this person carefully. You want someone who has a great natural energy and enthusiasm. Someone people really like a lot right from the start. It doesn't have to be the biggest and brightest star distributor in the Network. It's really best if this person is fairly new. That helps your guests relate to them better. Some people trot out their superstars right off the bat. I think that intimidates more people than it inspires.

The first speaker introduces him or herself and welcomes everybody. They go right into an enthusiastic presentation about Network Marketing. They let everybody in the room know what a fantastic business this is. How it's the wave of the future, the premiere business of the 21st Century—and how you can get into it today!

"Your Introduction" contains a lot of valuable information about our industry you can use here. I really wish there were a great book out there that explained our industry, its concepts and principles, and let people know about all the extraordinary possibilities just waiting for them in Network Marketing. It would be a terrific resource for distributors, especially in their presentations and in this part of the Opportunity Showcase.

What? Now *you* challenge *me*. You say, "Okay John, if you think that's such a great idea and so needed and so important, you write it."

Fair enough. I accept. That's what my next book will be about. A popularly written, mass market book that turns the whole world on to Network Marketing. Great idea. Thanks!

Now, after the speaker excites people about this business, he or she gets right into a lively sharing of his or her experience with the products and the opportunity. Short and sweet—a really warm, happy and compelling successful story.

Then this person continues with the following three key points they've been trained to speak about.

THE COMPANY, THE PRODUCTS, AND THE OPPORTUNITY

First, the speaker goes into the company itself. Give a general overview with a focus on the company's philosophy and success. Stay away from all the details and use stories whenever possible. Talk about the growth, number of distributors added, etc. Just paint a great picture of a powerful, successful, obviously well-managed, growing enterprise.

Next, the products or service.

Again, don't labor over details about each product or the technicals. It's an overview. The speaker's personal story and one or two stories he or she knows personally are best to share. (Here's another place that Story Box of yours comes in handy.) Hold up the product if you can. Just as with the company, make this part of the talk upbeat and successful—great products that *really get results* for people.

Now, talk about the business opportunity.

And, one more time, make it an overview and make it personal.

Have the speaker talk about how he or she started in

the business and what's happened for them so far. Have them share their expectations for the future as well. Let the audience see how enthusiastic they are, how they're already building and growing their business, and how inevitable it seems that the speaker will succeed—*in a big way!*

Throughout the presentation, have the speaker work from a flip chart—or even two of them—in the front of the room. This will add a graphic dimension to what's being said as well as help the speaker focus on getting his or her points across with enthusiasm and power. It's also a subtle way to let the speaker use the charts as an outline for the presentation, without having to resort to notes.

Show the Starter Kit and take the audience through all the benefits they get when they become a distributor. Mention purchasing the products at wholesale, the company newsletter they'll receive, the sales support material, and other tangible distributor benefits. Again, "Show and Tell." Take them through the initial investment and then give them a brief look at the marketing plan from the beginning to the breakaway levels. Don't go into detail. Most compensation plans are too complex to be understood in a short amount of time.

This first section takes 20 to 30 minutes.

ANY QUESTIONS?—YOU BET!

Your guest now has a pretty positive image of the company, products and opportunity. And, they've got some questions, too. Very important ones. Five of them to be exact. Here they are:

1. Is this business simple?
2. Can I have fun doing it?
3. Can I make money doing it?
4. Will they help me do it?
5. Is the timing perfect for me to get involved—now?

Answering these questions is the key to enrolling your guest into the business and jump-starting each one of your new distributors. It is the major objective of the Showcase.

So, how do you give them all the right answers? Thanks for asking. First, here's the hard way. Have somebody who's making $20,000 a month, who has been in the business for five or ten years get up on stage and say, "Look at me."

Why is that the hard way? Because most of your guests have a really difficult time relating to that superstar. It's a question of rapport.

Twenty thousand dollars a month is a quarter of a million dollars per year. What does a person who might take ten years to make that much money think of their chances of making all that in one year? At this point in their involvement with Network Marketing—Zip!

What does a person considering a part-time extra income who's got the most common fear of all, speaking in public, think when confronted with a full time, seasoned pro who's also a polished, relaxed super-communicator? "Not me, I could never do that."

As I said before, there are better places for the inspirational sales leaders to play a powerful role.

In the Opportunity Showcase, I like to use them at the very end or even after the formal part of the meeting. It really impresses people when you pull them aside and say, "How would you like to meet so and so? She's one of the top ten producers in the whole company, and she'll be one of your upline sponsors. She's one of the most incredible people I've ever met in my life. Come on, let me introduce you to her."

Now, that's powerful!

So, here's what I think is the best way to answer those important questions.

FANFARE FOR THE COMMON MAN

At this point, the speaker says something like:

"Folks, I've shown you all about the company, the products and the opportunity, now I'd like you to hear from some of our new people—men and women just like you who've been in the business only a couple of weeks or months. I'd like them to tell you what it's been like starting their (such and such) business. Come on up here and tell us about it."

The first speaker now turns into a traffic cop. People come up on stage, tell their brief one or two minute success stories, and sit back down with a big smile.

Now, these people are *trained* how to do this. That way, you're sure all those five key questions will be answered. Mix these people up—different shapes, sizes, backgrounds, approaches to the business, etc.

The important point is that they must answer those five key questions with their stories.

TRUE STORIES AND TRAINING

Now, I'm *not* suggesting people fabricate these success stories. Faking it doesn't work. Besides, nothing is as inspirational as the truth, and this business is so full of great personal success stories, you won't have to make them up!

I am suggesting that you train the people who are going to share so that they are sure to answer all five key questions. This is a must.

"Hi, I'm Norm Normal and I'm really excited to be here!"

"I got started with (such and such) two months ago. I tried the products and this and that happened and I feel terrific. So I joined with Natalie Networker who's been just great to me."

"Natalie showed me how everything works. She helped me send in my application and place my first order. Then she went with me to make my first few presentations and I made two sales and sponsored one distributor! It was great. I can hardly believe it—I never sold anything before!"

"I'm having a ball. I'm working eight hours a week, and this month my bonus and retail earnings made my car payment and bought me the portable phone I've wanted for more than a year now! Everybody's been wonderful to me. This is great. You gotta' do this. Boy, if I can do it—so can you!"

And Norm jumps off the stage to a round of happy, enthusiastic applause! Never forget the applause. No matter how many times you've heard Norm or anybody else for that matter. Give everybody the acknowledgment and appreciation they deserve. It makes a big difference to them and an even bigger difference for your guests. And even though you may not have guests that week, by appreciating Norm, you're ensuring his enthusiasm next week when you may have five guests.

I CAN DO IT, TOO

The point is simple—and very profound! What you want your guests to be saying to themselves is: "If he or she can do this, I know I can too." And if a couple of your sharing distributors say that out loud—so much the better.

Look at what's happened for your guests here:

They've seen and heard Norm and now they know the business is simple and fun—Norm made two sales and sponsored his first distributor his very first week. They know that they'll get all the help they need, because again, Norm said that's what Natalie did for him and she was just great! And they know they can make money too. Norm's realistic "… made my car payment and bought me a portable phone…" makes that clear as well.

And that last question, "Is the timing just perfect for me to get involved—now?" Norm gave that one a good shot too. His "This is great. You gotta' do this. Boy, if I can do it—so can you" lets them know that any time is the right time if it's what they want to do. And, if a good number of the success stories are coming from people that have been in the business only a few weeks or months, that in itself says that the timing is perfect!

After 45 minutes *total* are up—that's it. The speaker says:

"That's great! Thanks to everyone."

"That's it for the formal part of our Showcase. You're welcome to stay with us and chat. People will be available to answer all your questions. We have applications and Starter Kits ready for all of you who want to start your business tonight."

Now, please make sure to make the announcement of when the next Showcase will be given. Also, mention any special events—especially when the next New Distributor Training will take place. Encourage people to attend. Let them know it's a great way to get people started. And if they can't make it, encourage them to meet with their sponsor and have a one-on-one training session.

Have the speaker conclude with:

"Thanks again for being here. We appreciate you— and please, make sure to get all your questions answered. Goodnight."

The music comes back on. Hand your prospect an application and help them get started. Now is a great time to introduce your new distributor to some of the more successful, seasoned leaders at the Showcase. This acknowledges your new business associate and assures him or her that they did the right thing.

ABOUT TIMES AND DATES

Showcases are best on Tuesday, Wednesday or Thursday evenings. The best time to start is 7:30 p.m. sharp, with doors opening at 7:00 p.m.

I like to hold New Distributor Trainings on Saturday mornings, and with Thursday Showcases, it leaves only a couple of days before they go through training.

Now if your group is small enough, you may want to consider having the New Distributor Training immediately after the Opportunity Showcase. Take a 15-minute break and then get right into it.

You can do this training in about two to two-and-a-half hours maximum. Make sure to announce that you're doing a New Distributor Training right after the meeting. It makes for a bit of a long night, but it's a jet-propelled way to get people started fast and strong.

USE SYNERGY TO CREATE EXPLOSIVE SHOWCASES

Big meetings have one major advantage over smaller, more intimate ones. It's called *Synergy*. Synergy is a math term that describes the unique ability of a whole to be greater than the sum of its individual parts. The futurist, Buckminster Fuller, brought the concept of synergy into popular awareness, and created the following formula to explain it. (Please, bear with me and follow this closely. Once you understand it, you will have in your hands the most powerful Networking tool of all.)

Take the number of people present at the meeting and multiply that number by itself (or, the number of people squared).

Then subtract the number of people from that.

Divide the final number by two, and you have *the total number of relationships between all the people present*.

For example: if you have a home meeting and five people are present, it goes like this:

5 (# of people) x 5 = 25 - 5 (# of people) = 20 ÷ 2 = 10, which is the number of relationships between all the people present.

Even though there are only five people there, those five people produce 10 different relationships among themselves.

Now, let's put 60 people in a meeting and see how much synergy they've got together:

60 x 60 = 3600 - 60 = 3540 ÷ 2 = 1770.

That's one thousand, seven hundred and seventy relationships present at that one meeting!

Now, if the quality shared by each of those relationships is one of tremendous enthusiasm for the products, excitement and commitment to the company, and a genuine care and support of each other—what kind of energy will be in the room at the end of the meeting?

Powerful? You bet!

Synergy is the secret to the awesome power of Network Marketing. It explains how a Network Organization of as little as 1000 men and women can produce results that would normally require half a million people to accomplish. You can harness the power of synergy in every aspect of your Network Marketing business. (Especially to create dynamic and productive Showcases!)

It's time to learn what goes in your New Distributor Training Program. Are you ready? Great!

Chapter Ten:
New Distributor Training

All of the individual elements we've talked about—Goals and Purpose, Belief Systems and Prospecting, Presentations and Objections, and from Follow Through to the Opportunity Showcase—are parts of a powerful training system for fueling your successful Network Marketing business. In reading the previous chapters, you've probably gotten lots of great "Ah Ha" ideas. Now it's time to put them all together into a comprehensive New Distributor Training Program that will generate success for everyone in your entire Network Organization.

A s you know, I'm devoted to the idea (and the proven reality) that training is what really guarantees your success in this business—and by success I mean true and lasting personal and financial freedom.

Now, do you know what guarantees great training? Dancing.

Surprised? Let me explain.

Whether you dance with the Royal Danish Company—or in the company of Dan and Delores Danish down at Royal's Disco—what makes the way you dance really special, the kind everybody stops to watch and applaud, is *choreography*.

Choreography is how each step or movement interacts with the music and flows from one to the other to the next. The individual steps are your technique. Putting them all together in a continuous, dynamic flow—is your choreography.

TRAINING CHOREOGRAPHY

When you properly choreograph your own training program, your new distributors literally flow from one step to the next. There's nothing static or jerky about it, and this generates tremendous momentum for success, because each step builds on and leads to the next.

You start with their goals and purpose. Teach them to build a bonfire of passion and energy for accomplishment. Then you take them 1–2–3–4–5–6 through Prospecting, Presentations, Objections, Follow Through, The

Opportunity Showcase and Training their own new distributors.

Each of these "steps" flows right into the next one. And each of them is "hands on." Your new distributors actually make up their own prospect list, do the presentations, follow through with their own people, bring guests to the Opportunity Showcase and begin training their own new distributors.

They learn how to be successful distributors by being successful distributors.

This "do it" approach is so much more powerful than having them sit for hours while someone "tells" them how it's done.

By the time you get your new distributors through their first training "dance," they're ready to train their own new distributors. That's why this approach is so extraordinary. You haven't just taught someone how to do the business, you've taught them how to train others to do the business.

Talk about "earn while you learn!" Wow!

TIMING YOUR DANCE

Now good training choreography has everything to do with timing.

Remember, the Opportunity Showcase was on Tuesday, Wednesday or Thursday evening. Unless you worked with a small group and did the initial phase of your New Distributors' Training that very night, immediately after the Showcase, Saturday morning is the perfect time. This is one reason I like Thursday showcases best—less time until Saturday's Training.

SETTING THE STAGE

The very best suggestion I can give you is: *as soon as your prospect makes the choice to become a new distributor, give him or her a copy of this book.* Have your first act as a sponsor be to have your new business building associate read "Your Introduction" and the first two chapters— before you "dance" them through your formal New Distributor Training Program.

Remember how very important belief systems are. They are the "context" for the "content" of your training program—and for your relationship with your new distributor as well. That's why reading these chapters is so important. It sets the stage for your training program.

"Your Introduction" and the first two chapters powerfully cover the why of their new business. It helps them begin to fall in love with Network Marketing and recognize their business opportunity as the perfect vehicle to be, do and have all that they want in life.

So put this book to work for both of you—first. Have them read "Your Introduction" and the first two chapters—and complete the written exercises. This helps them establish their own goals and purpose and teaches them how to fuel their passion by using the four fuels: Visualization, Unshakable Faith, Education and Knowledge, and an Environment of Support. Once your new distributor sees the marriage between his or her goals and how your Network Marketing opportunity will help them achieve that, you've got one unstoppable new distributor to work with! Now that person is ready to sit down with you and others to learn the how-to's. And the time you now invest together will be so much more productive and rewarding for both of you!

If you can, meet with them (at least over the phone) to review their goals and purpose—before their formal training program. This gives you a greater connection and relationship with them. It helps you understand what's important to them in their lives, and gives you an opportunity to better support and empower them.

Now, let's get into the formal part of your New Distributor Training Program.

NEW DISTRIBUTORS NEED *NEW* DISTRIBUTOR TRAINING

I've said this before in Chapter Three, but it's so important that it bears repeating again. *New Distributors Need New Distributor Training.* And why not have new distributors train new distributors? If you use a well choreographed, hands-on training program, this is a snap. Too often people want to trot out the best and brightest "seasoned pros" to do the training. Just like in the Opportunity Showcase, a successful distributor who's been in the business for a number of weeks or months is better.

Why? Because they are initially more believable—and more importantly, they are duplicatable!

You want your trainers to be role-models. Enthusiastic, lively people others can learn from. Also, you constantly want to be training new trainers. When your organization is built on developing trainers, it will grow explosively. New distributors training new distributors, good strong trainers training trainers, and trainers of trainers moving up to positions of leadership... That's powerful Networking!

NEW DISTRIBUTOR TRAINING LOCATION

Home or hotel. Either one is fine. Just make sure the environment is conducive to a professional, working session of two to two-and-a-half hours in length. No pets. No kids.

Have a number of your newer distributors who've had some field experience at the New Distributor Training. They're a great help with generating questions and answers, brainstorming and sharing stories of how this or that works best. You can also have each of them do a section of the training program. It's a great way to prepare them for doing trainings themselves.

TRAINING WORKSHEETS

Have a pre-packaged set of handout materials for each person. Include information materials and the worksheets you're going to cover. Examples of some worksheets are in the back of this chapter.

If you cover things you want them to have notes for, I suggest you outline the notes and give them a copy. You cannot expect people to listen, absorb, practice and participate all at once. If you provide them an outline, they can focus on paying attention and being "present," instead of distracting themselves with extensive note-taking.

SHOW AND TELL

I mentioned that your training should be hands-on. Obviously, you will always be "telling" people lots of information. The key here is to make certain that you "show" them as well.

The best way to do that is to involve them directly in the process. That's why I use creative brainstorming and role-playing in all my trainings. To prove my point: when students are asked to complete an Evaluation Form at the end of our workshops—how do you think most of them answer the question... "What did you like most about the workshop?" You guessed it. Eighty percent or more answer... "The role-playing."

The various worksheets I speak about enable people to get directly involved in this process. For example, use role-playing exercises when talking about objections or the most common questions people ask about the product or opportunity. Rather than telling them what the benefits of the product are, let your new distributors come up with these themselves. This is a much more powerful kind of learning for three reasons.

1. *They will have done it themselves.* That gives them a real sense of ownership of the ideas.

2. *They will have worked together as a group.* Creative brainstorming and role-playing are fundamental aspects of active Networking. Now they know they can count on each other for creativity and support.

3. *Memory will increase tenfold.* If you just hand them a list, they've got to memorize it. If they make the list, they're much more likely to remember it.

THE THREE PART TRAINING

Your New Distributor Training is in three parts: First, we touch on Belief Systems, then The Product, next The Business.

Let's review the high points of each section. I've provided you with a mini-checklist of things you'll need for each phase. Please refer to each of the earlier chapters for more detailed explanations on each specific subject matter.

FIRST PHASE: BELIEF SYSTEMS (15- 20 MINUTES)
☑ Checklist
☐ Review Chapters One, Two and Three thoroughly
☐ Have success stories and testimonials ready
☐ Example of a Treasure Map

I talk about Belief Systems in Chapter Three. Chekhov said, "Man is what he believes." So true! Your new distributors have got to believe that they can do this business and do it successfully.

Remember when we spoke about what goes into an Opportunity Showcase, we said there were five questions every prospect needed to have answered before he or she could make a positive choice? Here they are again:

1. Is this business simple?
2. Can I have fun doing it?
3. Can I make money doing it?
4. Will they help me do it?
5. Is the timing perfect for me to get involved now?

Now, although you have covered these in the Showcase, drive them home again in the first phase of your New Distributor's Training.

Whenever possible, do it through success stories and testimonials. Share your own experiences and focus on addressing each of the questions above. Have some of the "seasoned" distributors share their stories and enthusiasm as well. This will give all your new distributors the proper, positive attitude and let them know they *deserve* success too. And make sure to acknowledge each of them for having the "Al and Alice Achiever" attitude and belief system.

If someone's willing, have them share their Treasure Map so everyone can see the power of pictures and vision.

To cover all of this material in detail, refer to: "Your Introduction"; Chapter One: "Your Goals and Purpose"; Chapter Two: "The Four Fuels"; and Chapter Three: "Training: Your First Step."

SECOND PHASE: PRODUCT OR SERVICE KNOWLEDGE (45 MINUTES-ONE HOUR)
- ☑ Checklist
- ☐ Review Chapter Four thoroughly
- ☐ Flip-pad, easel and colorful, bold marking pens
- ☐ Products for display
- ☐ "Product Benefits" worksheets
- ☐ "Commonly Asked Questions" worksheets

Simply stated, "You've got to be your own best customer." Again, remember how I spoke about the word *enthusiasm*. The last four letters of the word stand for I Am Sold Myself! And that's the key.

Product or Service Benefits Worksheet. Here's the first of your handouts. (An example is in the back of this chapter.)

Now it's time for creative brainstorming. Have your new distributors (and some of the "seasoned" ones too) call out some benefits.

Remember the distinction between features and benefits! We're after the results people enjoy, not what's special about the ingredients, or the special details of the product or service.

Write the benefits on the flip-chart in the front of the room. Also, take the time to have them write down these key benefits on their own worksheets. If you can, transcribe the sheet and give a typed copy to each new distributor as soon as possible.

Who's Most Likely To Use Your Product or Service. (This is a part of your "Product Benefits" worksheet.) When you get a number of men and women together from all different backgrounds, they come up with amazing ideas of who might enjoy the benefits of your product or service. I've been doing this for years, and I'm still amazed at how many new ideas come out of this. And how well it "feeds" new names for their prospect lists.

Commonly Asked Questions. More creative brainstorming and another worksheet. (An example is in the back of this chapter.) Get the most commonly asked questions written down on the flip-pad. Then go back and have the group brainstorm the answers. Some of your more "seasoned" distributors can help out with this. Now is the time to use role-playing exercises to anchor these well-thought-out responses. You can do the role-playing exercise in front of the group or create small teams.

In Network Marketing, more so than in conventional businesses, the company is all-important. So invest a little time talking about the company, its basic philosophy and its people.

Don't labor over this part. Much of what they need to know is in their distributor sales kit. Touch on it briefly and move into the next section.

All the information for conducting a successful second phase of your New Distributor Training program is covered in Chapter Four: "The Products."

THIRD PHASE: BUSINESS KNOWLEDGE (ONE HOUR)
☑ Checklist
☐ Review Chapters Five through Nine thoroughly
☐ Flip-pad, easel and colorful, bold marking pens
☐ "Prospect List" worksheets
☐ A sample Presentation Book
☐ "Objections" worksheets
☐ An example of a 3 x 5 card "Follow Through" box
☐ A Calendar of Events—Showcases and Trainings
☐ List of Showcase responsibilities—who wants to contribute?

Prospecting. Have a number of Prospect List worksheets as part of their handout package. (An example is in the back of this chapter.)

Coach them to fill out their prospect list, complete

with phone numbers. When you schedule the training, ask each new distributor to bring their personal and business address book. Encourage them to make their list l-o-n-g, and not to prejudge.

Prospect List Priorities. Show them how to set the three priorities for each name on their list.

#1. High-energy, people-people.
#2. Positive people.
#3. Successful people.

Let them know why you're setting these priorities so they can contact those prospects first that are most likely to say "yes" to a presentation.

Telephone Appointments. Teach them how to use the phone to schedule appointments.

Remember the five key points we mentioned:

1. Is this a good time to talk?
2. Transfer your enthusiasm.
3. Compliment your prospect.
4. Offer a disclaimer.
5. Close your objective.

Be sure to touch on how they work with prospects out of their area, using the money-back guarantee and other sales materials.

We covered all of this in Chapter Five: "Prospecting."

Presentations. Start by showing them different presentation books your distributors use. Teach them how their presentation book helps to guide them step-by-step through their presentation. This is the perfect time to set up an evening to work on creating presentation books together.

We covered this in Chapter Six: "Presentations."

Objections. This can be an emotionally "charged" topic. So, start by letting them know that objections are "opportunities in work clothes." Show them how to turn stumbling blocks into stepping stones by using the six-step process:

1. Listen
2. Be a detective—find the underlying question
3. Agree and appreciate the objection
4. Respond—use *feel, felt and found.*
5. Get confirmation
6. Give them a choice

These six steps form a powerful and effective system for deepening your relationship with your prospect and for having them make the very best choice possible!

Use an Objection Worksheet and have another creative session. (An example worksheet is in the back of this chapter.) People love this part, but what surprises them most is how easy and fun it is to discover and answer the real questions hidden in the objections.

You learned about this in Chapter Seven: "Objections."

Follow Through and Follow Up. Teach them how to use the 3 x 5 card filing system. Show an example of your card box, and walk them through the system.

This was covered in Chapter Eight: "Follow Through."

What's next?

THE OPPORTUNITY SHOWCASE

Have ongoing Showcases scheduled so everyone can bring their "hot prospects," to show them the big (first class) picture, and enroll them in the business. And as you've learned, it's vital to have personal or group New Distributor Trainings scheduled following each showcase, so everyone can start the cycle all over again. (If you can, have a calendar of these upcoming events to give to everyone.)

Using this (Showcase followed by a New Distributor Training Program) time frame, will allow you to build a strong Network Organization quickly and surely. Just do it yourself to experience how powerful it is!

WHO WANTS TO CONTRIBUTE?

The New Distributor Training is a great place to explain the purpose of the Showcase and give new distributors a chance to get involved.

There are many ways distributors can assist in putting on the next Opportunity Showcase. Something everyone can do is be prepared to share their story. That's the most important part of the showcase, and in the training you can coach everyone on how to make sure they answer those five key questions that are in every guest's mind. Here they are again:

1. Is this business simple?
2. Can I have fun doing it?
3. Can I make money doing it?

4. Will they help me do it?

5. Is the timing perfect for me to get involved now?

When your new distributors can tell their stories and answer these questions—your Opportunity Showcase will be an inspirational powerhouse!

For your review, this is all covered in Chapter Nine: "The Opportunity Showcase."

Whew! Seems like a lot to cover in a training program, doesn't it!

Actually, you can cover all of this easily and at a productive yet relaxed pace, in just two-and-a-half hours! It's true. You have to be a good manager and not let distractions knock the training off course, but I know you can do it.

During their first week, schedule as much time as possible to go with your new distributors on their first few presentations. I'll talk more about this in the next chapter on Duplication.

The truth is, with this training program, you won't have to go with them again, and again. The principles you're teaching them here build a foundation that is so solid, that many of them will be off and running quickly. Soon, they won't need you anymore. It's like children graduating from school and going out on their own. You've prepared them to succeed in the real world.

ONE FINAL POINT

Who's the best person to give a New Distributor Training? Everybody! In fact, everybody should.

Remember, Network Marketing provides us with greater personal and professional freedom than any other business system. We are the ones who are truly engaged in Free Enterprise.

As the Chinese sage says, "Yin and Yang: everything has two sides—a front and a back. The bigger the front, the bigger the back." *The front to our extraordinary opportunity is freedom. The back is responsibility. And the heart of responsibility is sponsor.*

Every Sponsor is a Teacher and Trainer, and every Sponsor can give a superb New Distributor Training. It's easy and fun. And the more trainings you do, the more you'll appreciate what I'm saying.

Take the checklist for each phase in this chapter and try them out. And when you see how it contributes to people, how it empowers them and literally propels them to achieve all they thought possible *and more*, you'll be hooked on training. Take it from me. I know!

And now for the big finish—Duplication!

PRODUCT BENEFITS WORKSHEET

"Why should people purchase and use my products?"
Use the following worksheet to help you discover features and benefits of your products. *People want to hear
benefits.*

Product or product line _____

_____

What benefits will people receive? (What is it for?)

_____

_____

_____

_____

_____

_____

_____

_____

_____

_____

Who's most likely to use it?
(Types and occupations of people) _____

_____

_____

_____

_____

_____

_____

MOST COMMONLY ASKED QUESTIONS

Question # _____

_____

Answer _____

_____

_____

Question # _____

_____

Answer _____

_____

_____

Question # _____

_____

Answer _____

_____

_____

Question # _____

_____

Answer _____

_____

_____

MY PROSPECT LIST WORKSHEET

Priority (A—B—C)

		Comments:
Name		
Address		
Day ( )		
Eve ( )		

		Comments:
Name		
Address		
Day ( )		
Eve ( )		

		Comments:
Name		
Address		
Day ( )		
Eve ( )		

		Comments:
Name		
Address		
Day ( )		
Eve ( )		

		Comments:
Name		
Address		
Day ( )		
Eve ( )		

OBJECTION WORKSHEET

Objection _____

Question in disguise _____

Response _____

_____

_____

Confirmation _____

Objection _____

Question in disguise _____

Response _____

_____

_____

Confirmation _____

Objection _____

Question in disguise _____

Response _____

_____

_____

Confirmation _____

Objection _____

Question in disguise _____

Response _____

_____

_____

Confirmation _____

Chapter Eleven:
Duplication

One of the most fundamental concepts in Network Marketing is Duplication. And with very good reason. Duplication is where "the rubber meets the road" for creating real and lasting success. One caution: duplication works both ways—positive and negative. In this final chapter, I'm going to give you a positive system for duplicating your training efforts that will enable you to create a truly extraordinary Network Marketing enterprise.

W ell, here you are. You've got a group of enthusiastic, newly trained associates just itching to get to work on their prospect lists! Wow! What an exciting moment. This is it!

Like they say on Broadway, "It's Show Time!"

But first, let's back up just a little before we get up on stage and take in all that well-deserved applause. Let's talk for a moment about this word, duplication.

DUPLICATION DEFINED

The dictionary defines duplication as: *to make an exact copy of the original; to do it again; or, to repeat.*

Duplicate comes from the Latin, *duplicare,* which means "to double." Have you ever heard of the "doubling concept" in Network Marketing? The doubling concept is usually applied to how your Network Organization grows.

You are one. You double and become two. Two doubles and becomes four. Four to eight, eight to 16. 16 to 32. 32 to 64. 64 to 128. 128 to 266, to 512, to 1024, to 2048 and on and on. That's the great growth possibility of Network Marketing.

WHY DOESN'T EVERYBODY DOUBLE?

Because not everybody learns that the key to doubling is the other double word—*duplication.*

The *only way* you will ever experience this doubling growth in your Network Organization in real terms— and by that I mean the kind that shows up every month on your print-out and on your bonus check—is by duplication. And just as duplication is the key to building an ever-expanding Network Marketing business—training is the key to duplication. That's why this is a trainer's training book.

THE WATER HYACINTH

I want to tell you a very revealing story about the power of duplication.

There is a floating aquatic plant called the water hyacinth. It grows on the surface of lakes and ponds in the tropics.

The water hyacinth grows by duplication. It doubles itself every day. One becomes two. Two becomes four, etc. Even in a big river or large lake, if conditions are right, within thirty days this plant can cover the entire surface of the water. No boats can cross. The hyacinth grows so prolifically, it simply takes over.

Now, here's what's so interesting. On day 29, just one day before the lake is completely covered—the lake is only half hyacinth!

That's right. Fifty percent of the lake's surface is water and the other half is hyacinth! And remember how the whole process began: with a little green plant no bigger than your hand! That's the power of Network Marketing.

In the beginning, it's hard to see how large your Network ultimately will become. When two become four and four become eight, that doesn't look like much in a vast lake that's all water. But envision down the road a bit—1000 people, then 2000, then 4000... And remember, the day before the water hyacinth completely covers the surface, the lake's half water. Awesome, isn't it?!

DUPLICATION WORKS BOTH WAYS

You can duplicate all the wrong things as well as all the right ones.

A recruiter who just runs around signing people up and then leaves them to their own devices, unsupported, poorly trained (or not at all), will duplicate themselves perfectly. They will end up with a Network Organization that does just what they do. Find them—sign them up—and forget them.

On the other hand, a Sponsor, who takes responsibility for the people they enroll in the business, who trains them and supports them, will duplicate themselves perfectly as well.

As you can see, one duplicates negatively, while the other duplicates positively. How do you choose to duplicate yourself?

DUPLICATION: THE POWER OF YOUR EXAMPLE

The process of positive duplication in Network Marketing is to present yourself as a model for others.

Remember the dictionary definition: *to make an exact copy of an original.*

Now, I'm not talking about "Send in the clones." Obviously, every person is a unique individual with values, character, goals, talents, etc., that are special to himself or herself. And certainly, one of the wonderful aspects of Network Marketing as a system and structure is how it naturally allows and enables people to express their unique individuality in their lives.

I'm talking about presenting yourself and approaching your business as a model of a system people can duplicate to create their own success.

Have you ever heard the term "turn-key" operation? It's used in the business world to describe an already set-up situation where all you have to do is walk in, turn the key, and it's up and running successfully. That's what you can achieve in your Network by being a duplicatable model people can use to build their own business—*just by turning the key.*

What's the key? New Distributor Training.

THREE WAYS TO MAKE MONEY

You can work for a job. That's what most people do. And there *are* jobs that are both fulfilling and rewarding. But the truth is, most jobs are just that—jobs—and you really end up working *for* them! They're something you do to pay the bills, and often that's about all you can do with them.

You can have money work for you. This is a wonderful way to make money, and it works great! With, say, $500,000 to $750,000 in the bank or in investments such as real estate, you can generate $5,000 to $10,000 in monthly income. Unfortunately, most people don't have an investment account like that. Someday I'm sure you will. For now, what are the other choices?

You can have other people work for you. Ta-Da! This is the one.

You use the proven principles of success and TST. That's Teach the Same Thing to other people. Then they do the same with others, and they do the same, too.

This way of making money has been used by the vast majority of wealthy people throughout the world. Another name for it is "residual income."

It's like our country's first billionaire—the late, great Andrew Carnegie said... "I would rather earn one percent from the efforts of 100 people, than 100 percent from the efforts of myself."

I believe in giving people a choice. So, which way of making money is right for you? Great choice. Now, it's time to learn how to duplicate yourself and have other people work for you—while they work for themselves.

TEACHING PEOPLE HOW TO FISH/ FLYING LIKE AN EAGLE

You're familiar with the famous saying, "If you give a man a fish, you feed him for a day. If you teach a man to fish, you feed him for a lifetime." That's what we're up to.

You want to begin setting a tone in your relationship with your new distributors where they're clear that you are teaching them to become independent business builders—not dependent ones. Here's an interesting example from nature that shows how that's done.

A female eagle selects a mate—a lifetime mate, by the way—and begins building her nest. She starts with strong, thick sticks and mud, which she uses like cement to form the foundation. Then she weaves the nest with lighter, softer materials, until she ends up with a comfortable, yielding, warm environment for her eggs. She lays the eggs, they hatch, and she begins feeding her chicks. I think she usually has only one or two baby eagles.

Then, an interesting thing happens. The mother eagle slowly starts to take out all the soft materials from the nest. She actually picks out the leaves and downy feathers and throws them over the side—so the nest becomes less and less comfortable. Then, when she thinks it's time for her young eagles to learn to fly, she starts pushing them out of the nest. She gently nudges them at first. Then the gentle proddings turn into solid shoves. If it gets to the point where, after a number of strong pushes, that baby eagle isn't getting the message, the mother picks it up and throws it out of the nest.

Now, as that baby eagle hurtles towards the ground, instinct rises to the occasion and the young bird flies. If by chance that doesn't happen, Mama swoops down, grabs the chick before it hits the ground, flies it back up to the nest, and after a reasonable time for rest and recovery, throws the baby back out again. And she'll keep doing that until that baby flies out of the nest on its own!

My point here is, if we want our new distributors to fly like eagles, we may have to throw them out of the nest.

CREATING INDEPENDENT BUSINESS ASSOCIATES AS QUICKLY AS POSSIBLE

You can be a star distributor in this business. There are lots of them. What I want you to become is a *star-maker*. It takes two things: you need to teach your people how to do the business, and, you need to teach them how to teach others how to do the business.

TEACHING HOW TO DO THE BUSINESS

First, sit down with your new distributors right after they've had their New Distributors' Training and set aside a block of time—say three hours on a weekday evening or three or four hours on a Saturday afternoon. This time is for them to have appointments with their key prospects. They can do it in their prospect's home or some other convenient location.

Now these meetings are one per hour every hour for the allotted time.

Your responsibility is to help them take their prospect list and set those first few appointments. Then you go with them to those appointments.

Have your new distributor introduce you as the third party expert. You are training your new associate so you make the first few presentations.

Since you have one appointment every hour, you must move along at a pretty good pace. Once you get your new distributor's prospect started on the product, review the 3x5 card "follow through system" with your new distributor and have them call these people reguarly. You can coach your new distributor and support them with their follow-up calls.

WHAT HAVE YOU DONE?

You've trained your new distributor, helped them establish retail customers and "jump-started" their business. Chances are also very good, you've assisted them in building their Network Organization by helping them sponsor their first few distributors.

Because you use a Presentation Book, after the first three to six appointments, your new distributor can do the presentation themselves. With all the elements they've learned in the New Distributor Training, each of your new distributors has both the information and experience to do the business successfully. Do you see how powerful this training system is?

In the fourth, fifth or sixth presentation, you sit back and speak up only if you're needed. Right off the bat, you've created a self-reliant business associate who knows just how it's done. Duplication—an exact copy of the original.

Three reasons this approach is so powerful:

1. It's lightning-fast. You're not waiting for the prospects to come to you. So in one day your new distributor has begun a successful, multi-faceted business career.
2. By approaching his or her prospects as a team, you dramatically increase your new distributor's chances of success in creating a customer and enrolling others in the business. And,
3. You've taught your new distributors *how to duplicate themselves.*

And you didn't just tell them, you showed them. They now have a direct experience of just how to do it.

Chances are, they'll be off in a matter of days doing the same thing with one of those prospects you just met with. *Big Al Tells All* by Tom Schreiter, is a great book for teaching this exact principle of teamwork and the third party expert principle. Tom has a wonderful, humorous way of relating the most common and self-doubt fears many new distributors go through when first getting started. It's fun, effective reading that really makes a special point.

TEACHING HOW TO TEACH

Here's a proven program that accomplishes extraordinary results!

First of all, this program lasts for one month. You pick one night each week, say Tuesday, and it's done in your new distributor's home.

Have your new distributor invite six, or eight prospects. Your new distributor does very little during the meeting, they simply welcome everyone and introduce you. It's like a mini Opportunity Showcase with you doing most of it in Week One.

Have a display of the products available and a distributor kit. Run the meeting just like a presentation using your own presentation book. The whole thing is informal. Don't re-arrange your new distributor's home. Conduct the meeting around the dining room table or around the coffee table in the living room.

You show the guests the product, share the benefits and your own experience. Here, your new distributor can share the benefits they have experienced by telling their own story. Be sure to answer those five key questions when you share about the benefits of the products or service and what it's like in the business. Remember: Is the business simple? Is it fun? Can I make money doing it? Will they help me do it? Is now the perfect time for me to get involved?

At the end of the meeting, make sure to tell all the guests you'll be back next week, same time, same place, and they are welcome to bring their guests—any family or friends—to the next meeting.

After the meeting, the new distributor follows up to make sure their prospects are well-serviced and satisfied.

NUDGE THEM OUT OF THE NEST

Now, next week, have your new distributor invite more new people. And this time, they do some of the presentation.

Have them take notes and tape the first session so they can study what you did. Then let them pick the part or parts they feel best about and have them do that in the second meeting. They can talk about the company, the product or service, etc.

Each week, your new distributor does more and more of the presentation—and you do less. By the fourth week, you are a special guest. Your distributor and possibly one or more of their new people, are the presenters.

GO AT YOUR OWN SPEED

No matter what your time commitment to your business, you can use these duplication structures of co-presenting and in-home meetings. The structure is the same. It's very flexible.

If you're a part-time business builder, you can do a meeting or two like this every week. You can work with one new distributor at a time.

A fast track approach is done the same way. It's just done with more new distributors and greater frequency.

Let me give you an example: the last time I was building an organization, I got to a point early on where I really wanted it to explode! I was willing to do whatever it took, and to make the personal commitments necessary to make it happen.

So, I went out and sponsored five serious business builders within one week. Then I scheduled this in-home program with each one of them for a solid month thereafter. That's Monday through Friday, one night each week working with a different distributor at each in-home presentation.

At the end of the month, I had duplicated myself with these five people and they were out starting to do the same thing with their own new distributors.

I immediately sponsored another five new business builders and started doing the same thing with them— training them, scheduling appointments and doing in-home presentations.

I did this for three months—ninety days. At the end of that short period of time, I had dozens of in-home presentations going on throughout the city—and I didn't have to be there! And at the Showcase once a month, my distributors would introduce me to their new people. I then began conducting advanced trainings for my established business builders, sharpening their presentation skills and teaching them how to manage larger and larger groups of people.

I also began to travel and "open up" new cities. That's when I saw the most wonderful benefit of this approach.

I would leave my home base for a month or so while I was establishing my business in a new location. Now, you would expect that my business would wane a bit in my absence. Instead, it increased! I had built such a strong Network of solid people who knew what to do in teaching and training their new people, that even without me, my business kept growing and growing. And that's the key.

Two important points here:

1) *I didn't stop sponsoring people first level.* This kept my business growing in both width and depth— and that balance is vital.
2) *This is a proven and practical process through which you can build both personal and financial freedom.*

Whether you work part time or, as I did, more than full time, the goal is to duplicate yourself so that you can have other people earning money for you whether or not you are directly involved in the day-to-day or week-to-week workings of their business.

Once this duplication system is in place, you support the men and women in your growing Network and continue to sponsor and train new people yourself. They will be doing the same thing. So will their people, and their people and their people.

And that's the point, not only in this chapter, but in the entire book. It's the key point in every single aspect of your Network Marketing business.

ALL ALONG THE WAY

If you train your people all along the way, their ability to duplicate your example is assured.

Their ability to teach and train others to do the same thing—is assured.

Their success—lasting, growing and ongoing in their business—is assured!

A professional gambler seldom takes an open-ended risk. He places well considered bets based solely on the odds at that given moment.

What teaching and training does for you in this business is:

1. It shows you and your new distributor clearly what the odds are. And...
2. It stacks those odds so far in your favor, you both can't help but win again and again and again.

Important point: If you have a new distributor that fights the commitment of time and money to be trained effectively, you may want to re-evaluate how serious that distributor truly is. Your time is valuable. Invest it with people who appreciate it.

HOW MANY PEOPLE ARE BEST
TO WORK WITH?

I say three to five at a time. Five is the maximum.

Look at the military. They've been teaching duplication for years and the chain of command is rarely more than five people. It depends upon the time you have committed to your business. More time—more associates. When you've completed training those five, you continue sponsoring five more, then five more, and so on.

And don't think for a minute that you have to sponsor hundreds and hundreds of people directly and train each and every one of them. My friends, there isn't enough time in any ten people's lives to do that!

The most successful distributors I know in this business have sponsored very few people.

It's true. One man who works his business part time makes $60,000 per year, drives a company provided Mercedes—and has sponsored 25 people first level in two-and-a-half years! He says, "I'm only interested in sponsoring leaders."

One Network Marketing millionaire I know who's been in the business 15 years and has a huge downline organization—has sponsored *less than 100 people*. That's only ten a year! He considers that fact the fundamental reason for his success.

Network Marketing may look like a numbers game. It is and it isn't. It's a "quality of relationships" game. Ten star-makers are worth their weight in gold. If they've duplicated themselves and made ten star-makers in each of their own organizations—and they will—you have 100 star-makers working for you!

REACH OUT AND TOUCH *EVERYONE!*

I have a challenge for you. I want you to have a $500 to $1000 monthly telephone bill!

"Hold on, Kalench. Are you crazy?!"

Not a bit. I want you to have a large phone bill and pay it effortlessly—without a thought. Here's why. Contrary to conventional Network Marketing wisdom, I believe you can and *should* sponsor people long distance.

Think about this for a moment. How old is Network Marketing? We didn't have many companies 50 years ago.

Yes, I know, we've had multi-level structures in conventional businesses, education and government forever. But not specific businesses based on the Network Marketing principles we use today. Ever wonder why?

The ancestors of today's Network Marketing companies were all the people who established "consumer-direct" businesses. Such as the Fuller Brush man who went door-to-door and others in the direct selling business. But what made Network Marketing come alive was new technology.

After the second World War, a wide variety of different technologies became available that changed the way Americans lived—and worked. The automobile, telephone, jet airplane and the copier were four big ones. Just imagine Network Marketing without the car, the phone, the plane or the copier?

Do you see what I'm getting at? Network Marketing exists by virtue of the advances in technology that enable and empower each of us to do this unique business.

Now, Network Marketers today have all kinds of extraordinary technologies available that simply weren't here yesterday. Fax machines, conference calls, overnight delivery services, voice mail, VCR's, audio cassette players, etc. And more and more leaders in this industry are using them.

The personal computer is only about ten years old! Think what a difference that's made.

So, the Networkers of today have all kinds of astonishing avenues of communication to exchange information, to prospect, sponsor and train people than ever before—and they can do almost all of this *at a very long distance*.

QUALIFYING YOUR PEOPLE QUICKLY

I know some sales leaders who teach their people to prospect using mostly state-of-the-art communication tools. An audio cassette that qualifies people as business prospects first. Only after a one or two-step business introduction, do these prospects learn about the specific company, products or services. This way, when the distributor sits down with someone, they are speaking to an already qualified business prospect.

As long as the tools are professional and ethical representations of the opportunity—I'm all for a system that gives serious business builders a prospecting edge.

THE KEY IS TRAINING AND DUPLICATION

With the proven principles and simple systems I've been teaching you, you can build a nationwide, even a worldwide Network. The only limitations are the constraints of your company's marketing agreements.

You can prospect long distance and follow through long distance. You can train by copying the required materials and teaching people over the phone what to do and say. You can use this book. You can send videos and cassette tapes. You can conference call. Every aspect of what I've taught you here can be done with people 3000 miles away!

Super Sales Leaders today are making tremendous use of the principles and new technologies available to us.

Company videos and audio cassette tapes enable you to be very productive at a distance. Conference calling is a stunning example of marrying the proven principles I've been teaching you with new technologies. Direct mail and advertising can work to interest and enroll people from all around the country—even all around the world.

No, you can't be with your long distance people at their Opportunity Showcase—at least not until they have a couple hundred people that show up each and every Thursday. Then you can fly in once a month. But you can use these principles, tools and techniques, and train your new distributors wherever they are. And you can do it simply and successfully.

The secret is giving a new technological twist to old Network Marketing methods. Take your phone, voice mail box, modem, fax machine, VCR, desktop publishing equipment, etc., and use them to duplicate what you've learned here.

It's what John Naisbitt called "high-tech—high-touch."

It's the future of Network Marketing, and it's your future, too.

Epilogue and Personal Note

LASTING WORDS

As a person on the path to being a Master Teacher and Trainer, I want to encourage you to keep company with other Masters.

Here is one from the East who has much to say in a few lasting words.

CHOOSE TO BE A LEADER

The ancient Chinese sage, Lao-tzu, put it perfectly—thousands of years ago:

I have three precious things which I hold fast and prize.
The first is gentleness; the second frugality; the third is
*   humility,*
which keeps me from putting myself before others.
Be gentle—and you can be bold.
Be frugal—and you can be generous.
Avoid putting yourself above others and you can become
*   a leader among men.*

A PERSONAL NOTE

I want to acknowledge you.

Before I do, I want to make sure you *really* listen to what I am about to say to you. So do me the favor of taking a long, slow deep breath or two and allowing yourself to relax fully.

Imagine you and I are sitting across from each other right now. Let's look at one another, eyeball to eyeball. I want you to know that I think you are a unique and special person. I know this for one reason—you've come this far in this book. To do that takes some qualities of which you may not be aware. And it's very important to me that you understand what a powerful, committed and already successful teacher and trainer I think you are.

I want to acknowledge you for making the time to read this book. For being either an Al or Alice Achiever. You understand the value of education and knowledge. Not everybody does. You are open to learning. You ask questions. You want to know the truth. These are all important qualities of a good teacher.

You love this industry because you truly understand it. Not many people do. You know that it's aligned with your purpose in life, and that it's a perfect way for you to accomplish many of your heartfelt desires and goals.

You know the power of making a difference in other people's lives. You know and you accept the obligation to share the gifts you have been given with others. And you know *why* and *how* to balance your freedom with equal responsibility.

Look at all you know and believe in. It's no wonder I say you are special.

Well, I want to challenge you. I know, I'm always challenging you. But I promise, this will be the last time—at least in this book.

I challenge you to *teach* every one of your new distributors so well that they surpass you. If the men and women in your Network are less than you are, you will soon have a Network of dwarfs. If they are greater than you are, you will have a Network of giants. It is the secret to the greatest success in this business and the secret I promised you would discover after reading this book.

Here is another.

A dear friend recently turned me on to a classic movie called *It's A Wonderful Life,* that stars Jimmy Stewart. Although it's a classic Christmas movie, I'd hadn't seen it before.

It's the story of a good and kind man, George Bailey, whose life's dreams and aspirations are smashed by a careless act that leaves him financially ruined. The town and his life-long friends have turned against him and he is on his way to a certain jail term. His miserable circumstances force him to choose between life and death.

He staggers onto the icy drawbridge outside of town with his insurance policy clutched in his hand. He is, he says, worth more dead than alive.

Just as he is about to throw himself off the bridge, a splashing, drowning old man cries for help from the river below. George rescues him, and as they are drying off together, the old man tells him he is his guardian angel,

Clarence, sent to him in his hour of need. George scoffs at this (in that wonderful way Jimmy Stewart has), but Clarence insists and tells him he has the power to show George how much his life is really worth.

He takes George back into a different life—one in which he was never born.

The entire town has changed dramatically—and for the much, much worse!

It's now called Pottersville, named for the cruel, rich tyrant who previously had caused the failure of George's Savings and Loan by stealing his money. There is drinking and gambling where there once were bright shops and parks. George meets the people from his real life, yet they are grossly different.

Without George Bailey having lived, an entire town and all its people lived totally different lives. Without George, hundreds, even thousands of people had become unhappy, hopeless and miserable.

Well, Clarence does get the job done. George chooses life over death.

And I watch with a lump in my throat as George races back to town, hugging the trees, kissing the ground, blessing the "Good Old Savings and Loan." He explodes through the door and calls for his wife Mary.

Mary, who has been out searching frantically for him, comes through the door and he sweeps her off her feet saying, "Oh Mary, I love you so much." And then it seems the entire town bursts into his house.

Everybody who had taken their money out of the

Savings and Loan in panic before, brings it back and piles it on the table. And everyone begins to sing Auld Lang Syne. Even the bank examiner, who just hours ago had demanded George's arrest, reaches into his pocket, puts $10 in the pile on the table and joins in the singing.

George glances down on the table, and there in the midst of the pile of money brought by all his friends, is a copy of the book *Tom Sawyer*. George opens it up and reads the inscription inside.

Dear George: Remember, no man is a failure who has friends.

It's signed, "Clarence."

Like George, you too have already made a profound and positive difference in the lives of many people. I ask you to think about those past contributions and acknowledge yourself for them.

Also, think about the future—and what it offers! The opportunity this industry and your company has given you is truly a special and powerful gift. I hope now more than ever, you recognize that power and see it as a means to even greater new beginnings and lasting contributions. And because you understand how to use it—*you possess that power and can now choose to unleash it.*

So, I want to acknowledge you for the commitment you've made to your company, your products or services, and your industry. Most importantly, I want to acknowledge you for the commitment you've made to yourself in *Being The Best You Can Be In MLM.*

It has been a privilege to serve you. I want to thank you for allowing me to do what I love to do more than anything else in the world—and for being one of my *one million friends.*

Your Friend,

John Kalench

ABOUT THE AUTHOR

"When I founded Millionaires in Motion in 1985," says John Kalench, "the Network Marketing industry had a very real need for a no-nonsense approach to education. Millionaires in Motion has come a long way in filling that gap."

A leading trainer, consultant and visionary for the Network Marketing industry, John Kalench was first introduced to Network Marketing in 1979. Over the next eight years, John built three highly profitable distributorships and was also the President, CEO and controlling stockholder in his own Network Marketing company.

In 1985, John was positioned atop a network of thousands of distributors nationwide. He created Millionaires in Motion (MIM) to provide specialized training programs for his network.

John's training programs were immediately embraced by his sales leaders throughout the country, and, in February of 1987, he decided to make MIM an independent training company for the entire Network Marketing industry. To meet this objective, MIM divorced itself from financial interest in any particular company— training and consulting would be its only business.

Since then, thousands of Network Marketing entrepreneurs like you have attended John's seminars and graduated from his workshops all over North America. Top sales leaders and company principals have also used his consulting expertise to better direct and expand their business strategies.

For two consecutive years, MIM received the President's award for training excellence from the MLMIA (Multi-Level Marketing International Association).

"The goal and purpose of MIM is simple," says John. "We want to be *Your* Network Marketing Training Company."

How to put the power of this book to work for you!

Everyone in your network should have a copy of *Being The Best You Can Be In MLM*. This book will inspire your people. It will focus their thoughts and energy and move them into a positive and committed plan of action. For those leaders that see the value and benefit of having such a proven source of *power* available to support them in building their business, the following volume discounts apply:

UNITS	CASES	UNIT PRICE	SHIPPING & HANDLING
1-5	—	$12.95 ea	*(Inside USA)*
6-11	—	9.95 ea	• All orders: add $3.50 or 5%,whatever is greater
12-23	—	8.95 ea	*(California residents add area sales tax.)*
24-43	—	7.95 ea	
44	1	6.45 ea	
132	3	5.95 ea	*(Outside USA)*
264	6	5.45 ea	• All orders: add $5.50 (U.S.) or 10% or actual freight, whatever is greater
528	12	4.95 ea	
1056	24	4.45 ea	

➡ **NOW AVAILABLE ON AUDIO CASSETTE!**

No time to read? No problem! Now you can listen to *Being the Best You Can Be* at home or on the road. These six audio cassettes are packaged in a sturdy, attractive album. **The product you asked for is now "hear." Only $49.95.**

Millionaires in Motion (MIM)
6821 Convoy Court
San Diego, CA 92111
(619) 467-9667

Phone order line:
1-800-388-1748
MasterCard & Visa accepted

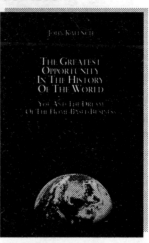

WOULD YOU LIKE TO GET YOUR MLM BUSINESS
ROLLING *FAST*? HERE'S HOW...

ONLY $69⁹⁵

YOUR *FAST TRACK* TO MLM SUCCESS

*A 90-day system that will turn your MLM business
into a high-profit, fast-moving machine!*

Are you ready to put your MLM/ Network Marketing business on the Fast Track? This result-oriented seminar has been conducted "live" for thousands of MLM/Network marketing entrepreneurs just like yourself. And now you can bring John Kalench into your home, car and network to be your personal MLM coach!

"Your Fast Track To MLM Success" is a powerful step-by-step system that will direct your energies and focus your actions to produce fast results in your business.

Incorporating all your learning senses to accelerate the learning process, you'll watch a 40-minute high-energy video that gives the key points and lessons of this proven seminar. You'll also listen to two audio cassettes of the full three-hour seminar, allowing you to turn your car into a "University on Wheels." Finally, you'll complete exercises in the "Driver's Handbook" that are designed to take what you have learned and put it into action.

Your investment is only $69.95 for the entire program and you have a full 30-day satisfaction guarantee It's easy, it's fun and it's powerful. Start now!

Call us now at 1-800-388-1748 to place your order. Use your MasterCard or Visa, or send your check or money order to:

> **Millionaires in Motion**
> **6821 Convoy Court**
> **San Diego, CA 92111 USA**
> **(619) 467-9667**

U.S. orders include $5.00 shipping and handling; outside U.S. include $10.00. California residents add your area sales tax.

"THANKS A MILLION FOR YOUR SUPPORT!"

Jeff Jordan	John Kalench	Tom Williams	Christine Elliot
Executive	*Founder &*	*Vice-President*	*Vice-President*
Vice-President	*President*	*Operations*	*Sales*

HOW YOU CAN SPONSOR JOHN KALENCH IN YOUR AREA

For only $10 (U.S.), Millionaires in Motion will send you a complete *Introduction Packet* that includes a 15-minute promotional video, a product catalog and information about our proven training systems. Also included are a list of training events and terms on how you can personally sponsor John Kalench in your city.

John can conduct a variety of exciting three-hour seminars and all-day workshops that will quickly and profitably accelerate your network's growth!

For any additional information on Millionaires in Motion's consulting and training services, please feel free to contact us at:

(619) 467-9667
6821 Convoy Court
San Diego, CA 92111

"YOUR NETWORK MARKETING TRAINING COMPANY"